MW01254561

<u>Successful</u>
Christian Television

Make Your Media Ministry a Reality!

by

Phil Cooke

ISBN: 1-4140-0569-5 (e-book)
ISBN: 1-4140-0570-9 (Paperback)

Library of Congress Control Number: 2003097585

This book is printed on acid free paper.

Printed in the United States of America
Bloomington, IN

Originally published under the title, *Producing Effective Christian Television Programs—Making Your Media Ministry a Reality*. This edition has been completely updated, expanded, and revised.

1stBooks - rev. 10/27/03

Dedication

This book is dedicated to everyone who's ever watched television or a motion picture and dreamed of using those tools to take a message of hope to an increasingly desperate world. And it's especially dedicated to my wife Kathleen and my daughters Kelsey and Bailey, who have sat at home on many a night when dad was in some remote part of the world helping churches and ministries achieve that dream. Without their prayers, patience, understanding and support, this book would have not been possible.

- Phil Cooke

Table of Contents

Preface

A number of years ago, I was invited to speak at a workshop entitled "How To Begin a Television Ministry" at a major national Christian conference. Some of the great pastors, teachers, and evangelists of our time were at the conference, and the workshop schedule boasted classes in evangelism, publishing, missions, counseling, Christian education, computer technology, and many other important areas.

When the time finally came for the television symposium to begin, I was surprised to discover that I was the only panelist invited who actually worked behind the camera. The other members of the panel were leading pastors, evangelists, and teachers, and each had their own television ministry, but I was the only representative of the production staff (producer, director, or other position) on the entire panel.

As the schedule worked out, I was the last person to speak, so I sat intently listening to what the other panelists had to say about starting a television ministry.

These pastors and ministry leaders all gave stirring messages on the importance of using the media to reach the lost. They spoke proudly of their broadcast ministries, and encouraged everyone to look to television as the future of evangelism. One even talked about how television is a great vehicle for house-to-house evangelism, since television is in almost everyone's living room.

All the comments were inspiring, but to be honest, they were all vague and general. Actually, most of the speakers spent their time talking about how their particular media outreach was a shining example of what ministries should be doing. But the fact was, they all left out something I felt was extremely important for that particular workshop—*practical advice on how to begin a television ministry.* As I looked out over the large audience (it was the most-attended workshop at the conference) I could see everyone's eyes glaze over. They hadn't come here for a series of sermons; they had come for *help.*

Just when most of the attendees where dropping off to sleep, I was finally asked to address the audience. When I stood up to speak, eyes started opening, and people began waking up. Not because I was a great speaker or a brilliant thinker, but because I began to give them *real advice*—the kind of critical television information they were looking for and desperately needed.

At the end of the workshop, they opened the floor to questions, and in spite of there being seven panelists, every single question was directed to me!

"Should I rent equipment or buy it?"

"How do I find a good producer?"

"Should I produce my program at the local TV station?"

"Will my Sunday morning service make a good program or should I use a studio?"

"How will I pay for it?"

"Where do I find equipment and crews?"

"Are there special techniques for preaching on television?"

When the workshop finally broke up, the other panelists filed out of the room, but I was swamped. The questions kept coming and coming, and I must have talked for another two hours to an eager group who would not let me leave.

That single workshop taught me that pastors, teachers, evangelists and other ministry leaders are starving for practical information about how to begin a television ministry. Thirty or more years ago, only a handful of prominent men with major ministries could afford to take a chance on television. But today, technology has changed to the point that nearly every church or ministry of any size can begin using television, radio, or the Internet in its outreach.

Many more experiences just like that workshop formed the genesis of this book. This information has taken me more than twenty-five years to accumulate, and it comes from years of experience, and thousands of questions from ministry leaders across the United States and around the world. I teach media conferences across North America, South America, Europe, and even Russia and I always encounter the same need for practical information. During the writing process, every time I decided to shelve the project, I met another pastor or ministry leader who asked me the same questions over and over.

I have discovered it isn't possible to cover every aspect of a television ministry in one book, and I haven't set out to do that. Rather, I have tried to focus on the most important questions you will face as you begin your journey.

Since everyone will be at a different level of experience in television, I have tried to concentrate on two specific needs:

1) Those who want to begin a television ministry and know little or nothing about the practical, everyday aspects of how to start.

2) Those who have experience, even years of experience, but for some reason can't seem to get the results they want. Perhaps they've reached a plateau and can't quite break through. Or perhaps they have a specific problem, but can't seem to identify its cause.

This book should answer many questions from each perspective. I firmly believe that even if you are currently producing a Christian television program, from time to time you need to go back to the fundamentals—*the basic, proven techniques for producing successful programs, to keep your skills vital and up-to-date.*

When I was growing up, my favorite football team was the Green Bay Packers. Coached by Vince Lombardi and quarterbacked by the legendary Bart Starr, they were invincible, and won enough championships to prove it. Coach Lombardi was a man who believed in the fundamentals—the basic techniques that every player needs to master his position. Even in preparation for the Super Bowl, a championship team still practices blocking, tackling, pass catching, and kicking—the basic, fundamental elements that can make or break a champion.

Today, Vince Lombardi's principles have been adapted by coaches and corporations, and many successful business principles have been created based on his philosophy of *mastering the fundamentals.*

This is your chance to get back to the basics—the fundamentals that create a solid foundation for your media ministry. I am constantly surprised at Christian television stations, program producers, and networks who seem to lack certain basic skills that would save them enormous time, money, and energy in their program production (not to mention enhance their program's effectiveness). But every champion begins with learning the fundamentals, and even the best start by mastering the basics.

Therefore, whether you're a novice or a more experienced producer looking for a refresher course, this is the book for you.

Above all, please understand that every ministry situation is different, and therefore flexibility is always important in consulting with any ministry on its television outreach. In many instances, I give different advice for experienced professionals, and offer various alternatives for other seasoned producers. But for most, there is no question that this advice is fundamental—proven, solid ideas and principles that will dramatically impact the success of a television ministry. In fact, don't take this to mean that there aren't any rules, or television production is a matter of personal preference. The fact is, there are very specific rules and principles that provide the foundation for media excellence.

I remember reading a great writer who said, *"The first thing is to learn all the rules. The second thing is to throw them out the window."* Most

Christian program producers have it backwards. In actual practice, only when you've mastered the basic techniques and rules can you creatively begin to explore new techniques and write new rules.

This lesson is critical because of the way television has impacted not only this country, but the world as well.

I was driving through the Oklahoma Panhandle some years ago and came across a sight that was so stunning I stopped the car, got out, and took a picture.

There outside a small town was one of the smallest, most ramshackle houses I'd ever seen. The yard had no grass, the roof leaked, it hadn't been painted in a decade, and it looked as if it might collapse at any moment. It even had the requisite car on concrete blocks in the front yard and the beat-up sofa on the front porch.

But sitting in the front yard in all its glory, was a huge home satellite dish!

At that moment, I realized the priorities of many Americans. They may not have a decent roof over their head, comfortable furniture, or paint on the walls, but whatever you do, don't deprive them of television.

With a country that places such a high value on the media, how can we not do everything in our power to try our best to reach those viewers with the gospel?

The debate over the media's place in America, and its good or bad effects on our lives is a wonderful debate, and I'm keenly interested in it.

But that's another book.

This book is for the Christian who has decided that current Christian programming could be far better, and who feels that God is moving his or her life and ministry in that direction.

As always, I highly recommend that before you begin to implement a media ministry, you continue to seek advice and counsel from the most professional sources. Bring in an attorney to help negotiate contracts for equipment or personnel; consult with an experienced media buyer before you implement a major airtime purchase; contact an experienced media consultant or producer before major equipment is purchased or rented; and on and on.

Television is an expensive medium. Don't take chances—get the professional advice and counsel you need. I will list some sources you might want to consider in the appendix later in this book.

I have always kept an image in my mind of a pastor, evangelist, or other ministry leader pacing the floor in the middle of the night, looking at Christian television or listening to Christian radio, saying to himself, *"I can do better than that."* If you feel that God is calling you to a media ministry, then you've made the right first step by getting this book. Now, I urge you to get out a pencil, make notes, mark it up, and underline it as you go. This book is designed as a *tool* that will help you develop a complete plan for your vision.

This advice would cost tens and even hundreds of thousands of dollars if you hired professional consultants. But now, perhaps for the first time, you have what you need to begin.

Now let's get with it.

Introduction

What is the first thing you think of when you hear the words "Christian television"?

If you have the nerve, ask several people on the street at random what *they* think. I did, and wasn't too surprised at the answers.

"*Beggars,*" said a rising young executive in his expensive suit. "*Every time I turn on the television and switch to a Christian station, all I ever seem to hear is a preacher asking for money.*"

"*Boring,*" said a teenage girl. "*I want something exciting that I can relate to, not a tranquilizer.*"

"*Patting each other on the back,*" said a middle-aged homemaker. "*I have a family with needs. My husband drinks, and I believe my two teenage daughters may be experimenting with drugs. I need answers to tough questions, not nice little interviews.*"

A Christian college student added, "*The quality of most Christian programs is so embarrassing. I'm ashamed to ask my non-Christian friends to watch.*"

The comments went on and on. Most expressed varying levels of frustration, a sense of being manipulated, and many expressed the opinion that the subject matter covered had absolutely no relevance to their lives.

It's common knowledge that only a small portion of the audience for these television programs care enough to financially support the programs themselves, and that includes people who watch these programs on a regular basis. Plus, research indicates that the vast majority of viewers of religious media are women, aged 55 or older.

But is Christian broadcasting in trouble? Is it floundering and even doomed to failure?

I don't think so, although I do acknowledge that it desperately needs direction.

In business, it's important to periodically re-think the nature of an organization and re-discover what the company is actually in the business of doing.

Although Nike is a multinational corporation, with business dealings and contacts around the globe, it's nevertheless important that Nike executives continue to realize that they are still *selling shoes.*

Other companies, although involved in a multitude of businesses, worldwide organizations and interests, have to constantly realize that they're actually in a very particular and focused business. In fact, many companies go bankrupt because they lose sight of that very concept.

That's exactly what Christian television needs to do. We need to sit down and re-think the nature of our calling, mission, and "business." (That's right—business—but we'll discuss that in a later chapter.) In spite of radically changing technology, satellite communications, global strategy, multi-national schedules and contacts, Christian media is still the simple act of *witnessing.* Sharing the good news of Jesus Christ with a world desperately in need.

But at the same time, it's witnessing on a dramatically different level.

Perhaps that's the great difficulty of finding real success in Christian television. Some understand the art of witnessing their faith effectively. Others understand the technology of global communications in the 21st century. But very few understand how to make both work together—especially now, as Christian broadcasting enters the "third wave."

Participating in the Revolution

Revolutions tend to have three stages.

The first is rooted strongly in spirit and emotion. It is driven by pent-up emotions and thwarted ambitions that expand until they are suddenly unleashed in such fury that even organized weaponry cannot stop the wave of "willpower" that explodes within the masses.

That stage has been seen most clearly in the relatively recent revolution in the former Soviet Union. In spite of the Kremlin's military might, political machine, and social engineering, the people had enough of Communism, and a generation of deceit was brought down in a matter of months.

The second wave of the revolution occurs when the conquest has been made and the need for stability takes over. That's the moment the skilled professional emerges. Details begin to be written down, plans are created, and strategy begins. The new order takes shape and begins to *function*.

That evolutionary process was the next step for the *new* Russia. Young entrepreneurs began taking hold, and the political process began undergoing dramatic changes, even though it was difficult to see how far the Russian people were willing to go to achieve true freedom.

The third wave is one in which "variety" begins to emerge out of the new and more stable order. No longer does everyone need to think alike, act alike, or feel alike in order for the new order to be effective or firmly grounded. Segments of the population begin to emerge with unique differences. "Market shares," "demographic profiles," and "audience diversity" become the coin of the realm.

Each stage of the revolutionary cycle is vibrant in its own way. Like the former Soviet Union, Christian broadcasting is standing on the brink of the third stage of its revolution, and to stay alive as a vital broadcasting force, it must seek greater diversity, quality, and vision.

In the late 1940's and early 1950's, a spiritual revolution took place across the United States. Few observers of history challenge that argument—a wave of evangelism and spiritual renewal flooded the land. Engaging and fiery Evangelicals like Billy Graham and Pentecostals like Oral Roberts traversed the country, packed in the crowds, and changed the religious landscape forever.

The mainline and traditional churches had become stagnant for the most part, and Americans flocked to hear and watch the young evangelists who packed sports stadiums and gospel tents from town to town. They spread out their sawdust, set up the tents, and preached with sweat rolling from their foreheads on hot, dusty summer nights and tens of thousands responded.

In the 1960's and 1970's, the evangelists began to rent plush auditoriums. Fans gave way to air conditioning. Tambourines gave way to electronic music and tape recordings. And fervor gave way to skill, not entirely, of course, but certainly audience expectations had risen by this time to the point where the preachers and musicians needed to be more polished, with more elaborate sound systems, in order to be heard without criticism.

In some ways, evangelism had become a "technique" nearly as much as a "calling."

But those changes paved the way for the great variety of evangelistic outreaches on the scene today. Evangelists, teachers, drama groups, music outreaches, street ministries, men's and women's ministries, urban outreaches, and more are reaching out today as never before. A great deal of evangelistic effort occurs in small "cell-groups" within large churches, in "praise groups" within traditional churches, and in one-on-one ministry within other settings. As that wave evolved, we discovered that one need not be a "famous personality" in order to be an effective evangelist, or to demonstrate spiritual gifts.

Although a number of pioneers ventured into Christian television in the 1950's and 1960's, the real revolution of the media began in the late 1960's and early 1970's. At that time, the innovators knew little of television technique. They operated largely on fervor. And since television audiences knew nothing of what to expect from "prime-time religion," many tuned-in out of curiosity. Millions were swept up in the emotion of the event and became names on huge mailing lists. Across the country, Sunday morning—once the haven of farm programs, pork belly reports, and local shows—began to fill up with religious programming.

Over the next thirty years, the general television audience became increasingly sophisticated, and so did the programs they watched. The public, including the "Christian TV viewer," was becoming visually literate. They demanded greater and greater sophistication in the programming, from more professional camerawork to better musicians and more interesting content. And what was true for the general populace was also true for the *Christian* viewer. During this same period, Christian television programs became more sophisticated, more professional, and more technically refined.

We are now on the brink of the *third wave*, in which diversity and variety are going to become more and more important. As I write these words, my cable television company offers more than 500-channels of programming. Once thought to be an impossible technical achievement has now become commonplace.

500-channels.

I can now see multiple sports, music, movie, kids, and religious channels, and I even have channels devoted to entertainment reporting, documentaries, and multi-cultural programming. In this media environment, individuals are going to need to find a niche and fill it— and fill it effectively.

Incidentally, *effective* is the operative word for all that we will share on the following pages of this book. After all, if it isn't effective, how can we possibly justify the incredible expense and effort?

Effectiveness

I was recently asked to consult with a church organization on the possibility of their producing a local television program. As I walked into the beautiful facility, I couldn't help noticing the great amount of printed material the church had created. They had "Prayer Request Forms", "Visitor Information Forms", leaflets advertising special events, pamphlets on a wide variety of programs within the church—the racks were literally filled to overflowing with literature.

I asked the pastor, "Isn't all this expensive to produce?"

"Confidentially, we're about to go broke over it," he said. And before I could respond, he added, "But it makes this church look so effective."

Look so effective?

That kind of extravagance is impossible in television. The equipment is so incredibly expensive, and the cost of production and airtime so great, that to do something "just for show" or "just to impress" is a ridiculous waste of time.

Sooner or later, your bank account will run dry.

A television ministry *must* be effective in order to survive. The long, sad list of failed Christian television programs and ministries is tragic testimony to that unassailable fact.

So what do we mean by *effective?*

To be effective, a program had better reach an intended audience, with a message that matters to that audience, and gets results.

In certain cases, it means to get results to the extent that the audience is willing to financially support the program.

You may ask, "What about programs and movies that have been made with a great message but never made any money?"

That is the great irony of producing anything creative—from books, to television programs, to recordings and motion pictures. It goes without saying that there are outstanding ideas and programs that will never find a large enough audience to pay for them. You see this every year in the race for Academy Awards. The movies the critics pick as profound commitments to the art of film are often shunned by mainstream audiences. Classical works of music and literature are rarely the best sellers. We've even created two markets in most media—the "art" market and the "popular" market.

There are some cases in the Christian television world for instance, where large churches have made a commitment to finance their pastor's television program and he never has to depend on ratings, income, or direct mail results. That's a great situation to have, but it's a rare luxury. In those cases, the producers can afford to be extraordinarily creative and explore controversial areas, without fear of alienating a segment of the audience. Evangelism can be a great priority in those ministries because producers don't have to worry about raising money or offending the audience. They can devote the entire program to reaching the audience with the intended message and without compromise.

That's why it's an important distinction to note that *how much response a program gets isn't the only indication of its success.* Frankly speaking, there are some very poorly produced programs on the air in both secular and religious arenas that are a tremendous financial success. On the other hand, there have been some outstanding efforts that from a financial and/or ratings viewpoint have failed miserably.

One of the great examples in the movie world is director Martin Scorsese. By most critical benchmarks, he is celebrated as one of the most gifted and brilliant filmmakers of his generation. Although he certainly does not make "family entertainment;" his movies, which often explore the mean streets of New York, are powerful examples of storytelling on film. To most critics, he is simply an American treasure, and since the 1970's, his films have defined excellence in movie making.

But his box office results are amazingly low. His films are almost always a hit with critics, but a miss with the mass audience.

Quality is important, but it isn't always an indicator of the program's potential success.

Paid Time Programming

Today, most Christian television programs are called "paid time" programs. That simply means that instead of finding sponsors to advertise during the program, the church or ministry buys the time slot outright and pays for the airtime. Some use that broadcast time strictly as a ministry, and raise the money in other places. Others use giveaways and product offers to get names for mailing lists, and still others ask for money directly during the television program. For most, it's a combination of all of these factors.

We'll discuss some of these options in a later chapter on fundraising. This book isn't the place to discuss the pros and cons of sponsored time versus paid time broadcasts. But you should know that there are innovative TV stations and producers working right now, experimenting with other financing possibilities for Christian programs. At this moment, it's important that you at least know the typical situation you'll find when you try to broadcast your program.

In the best of all possible worlds, we could produce the finest programs and not ever have to worry about where the money comes from. But in reality, you will probably have to raise financial support for your program, and to do that, you will need to view *effectiveness* from that perspective as well. Certainly there is value in the aspects of your program that won't generate a financial response. But you will also have to keep track of and understand the aspects of your program that will.

You may well spend the rest of your television career in search of that incredibly important balance.

But without it, everything else is just pointing cameras in the dark.

Chapter One

Starting at the Beginning

"Why do you call me, 'Lord, Lord,' and do not do what I say? I will show you what he is like who comes to me and hears my words and puts them into practice. He is like a man building a house, who dug down deep and laid the foundation on rock. When a flood came, the torrent struck that house but could not shake it, because it was well built. But the one who hears my words and does not put them into practice is like a man who built a house on the ground without a foundation. The moment the torrent struck that house, it collapsed and its destruction was complete."

Luke 6:46-49

"You can't hit a home run unless you step up to the plate. You can't catch fish unless you put your line in the water. You can't reach your goals if you don't try."

Journalist Kathy Seligman

Throughout this book, for purposes of brevity, we will be taking certain things for granted. For instance, that you're starting this venture with some sense of calling.

A calling of purpose, of mission, of destiny, and of divine assignment.

Whenever I speak to conferences, seminars, or workshops on religious television issues, I always make sure they understand that the *calling* or the *anointing* is something entirely out of my realm. I can teach production techniques, creative ideas, producing and directing, preaching techniques, and more; but the calling on your life and ministry is between you and God.

While that sounds obvious, it's important to understand because throughout this book we'll be dealing with the real-life, practical aspects of religious television. You can learn them, implement them, and use them to perfection, but unless God has genuinely called you into a media ministry, then I don't predict much success. We're all born with specific gifts, talents, and callings; therefore, this is as good a time as any to re-examine the calling God has placed on your life.

In Christian churches and ministries, that purpose is generally evangelism or teaching and training people in Christian doctrine, concepts, values, and behaviors. At least those are the only "passions" that I have encountered that seem to have staying power in television ministries. Whether you teach serious doctrinal and theological issues or more practical, everyday life-skills, these programs help people understand their relationship with God and the Bible, and how it impacts their daily living.

There is, of course, a completely different side to Christian television—that of television *entertainment*. Many Christians are skeptical of entertainment, and I've talked to those who consider entertainment some type of low-class endeavor. I, on the other hand, think that much of what is wrong with mainstream television, movies, books, and other media today is that Christians walked away from "entertainment" decades ago and left that arena to the enemy.

Now we complain that we can't find any good family art, movies, TV shows, videos, music, magazines, etc; and I place much of the blame at the feet of the Christian community. It's because we gave up that territory years ago that we wonder why Satan has such a strong hold on it today. The fact is, our retreat from that arena can be traced all the way back to the Protestant Reformation. Before the Reformation, the "Church" (what we now call the Catholic church) was a strong supporter of the arts—painting, sculpture, music, and drama. When you travel throughout Europe today you can see the lasting examples of a church that supported artistic expression as you tour the great cathedrals and museums.

Few people realize that the early church usually had three people read the scripture as different characters during worship services. They knew that scripture was not some ancient, dead book, but the living Word of God that was created through the drama and stories of human existence. Therefore, they felt that to fully express these stories it should be read by groups of people in a dramatic form. For only one person to read the scriptures publicly was to bore the audience and render it in less than its full dramatic presentation.

Later, what we call "mystery and miracle plays" during the Middle Ages were great church pageants and dramas depicting Biblical scenes and stories. These church dramas were so popular and became so elaborate, they exploded from inside the churches, spilling into the streets, where they toured Europe as a great teaching lesson on morality and Biblical values. The history of how Christians have used diverse artistic forms throughout the centuries would surprise and shock most Christians today.

But the reformers were so intent on destroying any vestiges of the Catholic church, that during the Reformation, much of the church's artistic expression was tossed aside along with Catholic doctrine. There is no doubt that the reformers made significant and important theological changes that resonate still today. However, in their wake they also went too far in their absolute determination to change the direction of the church—particularly in the area of the arts. For example, thousands of paintings and sculptures across Europe were destroyed, some only surviving because they were designed into the building, so that destroying them meant the building might collapse. And even more significant for Christian worship, as you look at the great cathedrals of Europe, you'll find most are designed in the shape of a cross. At the center, there are great altars where music, liturgy, and drama can be performed as part of the worship. But after the Reformation, when a new church was built, it was designed as an *auditorium*, where the pulpit became the focus of the building. Great for preaching, yes—but not so great for music, drama, or liturgical expression.

Our lack of compelling faith-based music and drama, especially in the secular world, harks back to these tragic changes in our thinking. I happen to be a very strong proponent of high-quality Christian entertainment programs, and have geared much of my efforts in that direction. One day, I hope to write another book on that vast and needed subject.

But for the purposes of this book, we are going to look at the *ministry* side of television—producing programs that will have a direct effect on the salvation, the training, or the general motivation or encouragement of people.

Granted, many of the techniques you learn in this book will work on either side of the industry, but for now let's focus on what is generally considered "ministry" oriented media.

Passion and Calling

Just because you occupy the position of pastor, teacher, evangelist, or television writer, director, or producer, does not mean that you feel a burning commitment within you, a *calling* that has branded your soul and from which you cannot escape. I'm talking about all-pervasive *passion*—not just ambition or enthusiasm.

I emphasize that word, because if you don't have a mission burning a hole in your soul, you probably don't have the inner fuel and fortitude necessary to sustain a long-term media ministry. When the hours get long, when the camera breaks down just as you reach the peak of your message, when the director demands just one more "take," when words won't flow from your mouth to your satisfaction, when you just can't seem to get your audience to respond, you'd better have a reserve of strength upon which to draw. You'd better have that deep-down, rock-bottom foundational sense of destiny, purpose, mission, or assignment—or you simply won't make it.

Stay with me now. This chapter is going to get serious, and some might even find it tedious or frustrating. But it's critical to walk through these steps before we begin the journey to a media ministry.

If I were sitting down, face-to-face with you right now, I'd grill you on these very points:

What do you feel compelled by God to do in the media?

When did it begin?

Why do you feel that calling?

How would you feel and what would you do if something suddenly happened so that you could not fulfill that mission?

In my experience, I've found that those who truly have this depth of commitment and calling are always capable of verbalizing their call succinctly. In writing motion picture screenplays, we use what is called a *log line*—a short, one-sentence description of exactly what the film is about. In Hollywood, it was started to fill the tiny slot in a typical TV Guide or movie review. Your concept may be the most complex motion picture of all time, but if you can't distill it down into a simple description, then you don't really know the story. Perhaps the classic Hollywood log line was for the science fiction thriller *Aliens*, which was *Jaws in space*.

It's not that different in reference to your ministry. In fact, I would invite you to take this very practical test of your own sense of purpose:

Write down in 25 words or less your mission and your calling.

Don't write it in general terms like "I feel that God has called me to win the lost," but in *specific* terms that would explain why God has called someone of your exact talents, experience, and desire to fulfill this dream through the media.

Before a businessperson asks for a loan he or she has to write a business plan—a detailed account of what the purpose of the business is, where it's going, and why. That plan is often used by banks as a basis for their lending decisions, and few investors will even consider a proposal without a proper business plan attached.

It may sound a bit trite at this point, but considering that you're going to easily spend hundreds of thousands of dollars in pursuit of a television ministry, taking the time to focus your sense of calling isn't too much to ask.

Take a moment right now to write your statement, and then re-read what you have written. Do you want to change any part of it? Add something? Subtract something? I suggest that you leave this material for a few hours—perhaps even overnight or for a few days. Let your words cool.

Simply take a break from this book to think and pray about what you've written.

Then, read your words again.

If it's absolutely impossible to write this type of description of your call, don't be discouraged. It doesn't mean you don't or won't have one. However, I do recommend that you diligently seek God about this very issue. The tough-minded determination that comes with this type of calling is absolutely essential for the successful pursuit of a media ministry.

One minister often says, "I can't promise you overnight success, but I can promise you day-and-night success. When you are willing to pursue something with day-and-night energy and enthusiasm, you'll generally find what you are looking for."

I believe that if you seek God for a sense of purpose, direction, and mission—and you do it with day-and-night diligence—you'll uncover a vision that thrills your imagination and ignites your passion.

But a calling isn't all it takes to have a successful television ministry.

You also have to have a deep desire to be on television. Not an egotistical desire to see your name in lights, but a deep conviction that television is the best way to deliver your particular message.

There are many ways in which you can fulfill a burning call of God on your life without standing in front of a television camera. Television is a technique, a vehicle, a method for getting a job done. In this context, it is not necessarily an "end."

It is a "means".

Do You Really Want a Television Outreach?

- *Or is television an aspect of ministry you just would like to have?*
- *Or is it something you think you should have because your church is large or because significant members of the congregation are behind the idea?*

- *Or do you feel it's time for your ministry to grow to a national or international level?*

The media exacts a high price. It doesn't happen easily or cheaply, and it doesn't happen without a great deal of energy being spent. Do you really want to be on television or radio?

Really?

Are you willing to learn the techniques required to be successful on television or radio? Are you willing to learn new skills? Are you willing to change some of your existing ways of communicating? Are you willing to change your presentation as audiences and culture change?

The message never changes, but the methods do. You're presenting a God who never changes, but if your *presentation* never changes, you're in trouble. Look at television over the course of your own lifetime. Can you see how programs change, styles change, music changes, and people change? Get used to change. If you're going to be successful, change will become your best friend.

Do You Really Desire a Media Outreach?

To begin an effective media ministry, you need to acquire techniques and knowledge about the specific medium in order to be successful. You can't substitute skills for passion about your calling or about the medium. Neither can you substitute passion for skills.

9

(Would you submit to a major surgical procedure performed by someone who loves you, but has no medical training? Probably not. Neither would you submit your life to a highly trained and qualified medical doctor who had absolutely no concern for you or your health.)

While I write this book, I've been having serious discussions with the leader of a major international ministry who believes it is impossible for *professionals* to be anointed for Christian service. Instead of professional camera people, directors, lighting technicians, or other crew members, this ministry leader hires only from within the organization. As a result, the ministry uses camera people who are normally mail room sorters, directors who are normally phone counselors, and producers who are former construction workers. They all love the ministry and exhibit loyalty, dedication, and commitment. But without exception, their skills in television are zero.

Needless to say, the television outreach has some serious problems.

Certainly, there are professionals who don't understand Christian principles or motivations. But there is also no question that a dedicated Christian, trained in the principles of media excellence, can strike a powerful blow for the Kingdom.

Take the time to become informed. Read about the television industry in general and about television as a medium. In the appendix of this book, I have included two sections. One is a list of practical resources to help you learn about the everyday production of television programs. The other is a compilation of books that will teach you about television's role in our culture and the impact it has on an audience. It's important to not only understand how to produce television programs effectively, but to understand the media's role in shaping the culture and the behavior of others.

One of the greatest sources of information is to talk to those already in the industry. Develop relationships with other pastors or ministry leaders who produce television programs you admire. Get to know people behind the scenes. The more perspectives you can get on the process, the better.

Simply put, seek the best advice you can find.

Several years ago, I met a minister who said that he felt led to use television to reach a specific region of the nation with the gospel. He insisted on producing a "live" daily interview and ministry program that he felt sure would be successful.

He had a calling.

He had a passion for ministry.

But he refused to look squarely at the facts surrounding his situation. He believed that he only needed to launch out and that any problems he encountered would resolve themselves as God intervened along the way.

Before long, he began to realize just what it took to have this kind of television program. He faced the tremendous job of hiring a crew that was qualified, enthusiastic, and willing to make the commitment of energy that a daily program requires. That commitment included securing a studio, booking guests daily, and paying the bills that turned into a mountain even before the first program was broadcast.

He hadn't counted the cost.

11

Eventually, he retreated from the idea and dropped the program, with considerable loss of confidence by his financial partners (to whom he had boldly declared that this television program was God's will for his life). It also resulted in a great deal of debt and financial embarrassment.

To have a successful television outreach, you need to be willing to "pay your dues" by getting good information, personal training, seeking the right counsel, and anticipating all of the risks and costs involved in production of a show.

The High Price of Manpower

Not only are staff members uniquely skilled, and therefore *expensive* to hire in terms of salary, television is a ravenous animal that chews through scripts, program ideas, music, guests, and preaching material faster than those elements can be shoved into its mouth. The pressure of creating enough material to feed the beast can be enormous, and many times I have seen producers, directors, and writers just throw their hands in the air and quit—or perhaps more commonly, produce highly inferior programming that keeps the show on the air, but only as a shadow of its real potential.

The High Price of Equipment

Ministries tend to go to the extremes in their approach to equipment and its cost. There are those, on the one hand, who nearly faint the first time they hear the cost for purchasing (or even renting) the necessary equipment to produce a quality broadcast.

And there are those who rush to purchase equipment even before they have a proven idea for a program. Years ago I met a minister who had spent nearly $650,000 on a post-production facility (editing equipment) before a single program had actually been produced and broadcast. In other words, even before they knew if the idea would be acceptable to the public they intended to influence, even before they knew if they would personally be able to "perform" to expectations, even before they were fully settled on the right format for their purposes, they were rapidly on their way to spending a million dollars in equipment they might never need!

The High Price of Errors

As recently as twenty years ago, television equipment was prohibitively expensive to own, bulky to handle, hard to maintain, and difficult to operate. But the same advances that have enabled hand-held calculators to flourish and computers to be available in most homes in America, have worked their magic in the television industry.

For years, the heart of a television camera was a system of electronic tubes. The most aggravating aspect of camera upkeep was constant *registration* or alignment of these red, green, and blue tubes, which together gave the full color spectrum to the camera. A trained and usually expensive video engineer was a necessary staff member. His

13

or her job was to manually adjust the camera electronics before each program.

Later, as technology developed, and with the advent of the internal computer, the registration sequence could be done automatically. And today, the computer chip allows the camera to electronically generate coloration. Cameras are simpler to use, more rugged, and no longer have as many adjustable parts to fall out of alignment.

Today, digital video cameras costing little more than a thousand dollars create better pictures than a hundred thousand dollar camera of 25 years ago.

Camera technology is just one slice of the television equipment pie. But I use this example to illustrate an important point: *in using finances wisely, you must make purchases that stay abreast of technology* and allow for one component of your system to fit with all other components. You may be able to buy a home stereo system without needing to know a great deal about audio technology, but you'll get into major financial trouble if you attempt to build a professional radio or television studio assuming that all of the pieces will automatically fit together—today or five years from now.

Television and Radio are Financially Unforgiving

Years ago, a dynamic young evangelist with a growing ministry decided to produce a prime-time television special. *Prime-time variety specials* were a favorite of the networks in the late 1960's and early 1970's, and for years they were some of the most popular programs on television. Jackie Gleason and Red Skelton achieved legendary success in this area, as did John Denver, Donnie and Marie Osmond, Carol Burnett, and later, Barbara Mandrell. In ministry circles, Oral Roberts was the pioneer in using prime-time family-oriented variety specials to present the gospel, and in the 1960's and 1970's he reached some of the largest audiences in Christian television history.

The young evangelist went to the expense and time of booking a popular singer who had experienced a great career as an entertainer and had recently been converted. He then had music composed, prepared a preaching segment for the program, and hired a first-class technical crew.

What went wrong?

He hired a producer who had no understanding of what I would call the *state of the culture*. The producer made entertainment more prominent than ministry. The script was weak, and demanded dozens of overtime (translate—*expensive*) hours to fix. The delays created an unhappy and very cranky live audience.

But most importantly, the producer didn't understand that the "prime-time variety special" format was already going out of style. When the program was completed—way over budget—it failed to get the entertainment and ministry elements into balance in the editing room, and coupled with an out-of-date format, was never broadcast.

The television stations gave it a very cool reception since it was so out-of-fashion, and they quickly realized that to throw more money away buying expensive airtime would probably bankrupt the ministry.

15

As it was, it took more than two years for that ministry to financially recover.

Television Can Be a Tough Sell to Supporters

Although prices are constantly fluctuating, the average man on the street cannot comprehend that a single television camera for a network-quality program can cost $50,000 - $150,000. Even more importantly, the average ministry supporter has little understanding that ministries must buy television station time in order to broadcast their programs. They simply don't think about it, and if they do, the likelihood is they have no concept at all of the enormous cost.

Lest you think that pastors and ministry leaders today are much more sophisticated about television, I still receive inquiries from ministries asking about the possibilities of finding free prime-time slots on stations around the country!

What Then is Our Conclusion to This Matter of "Getting Started"?

1) Make sure that you have a distinctive call of God on your life that you can articulate, and that you are willing to pursue with the full force of your energy.

2) Make sure that media is the right method for fulfilling that call of God on your life.

3) Make sure you get good information and are willing to take the time and pay the price for acquiring reputable advice and proven skills for yourself and your associates.

How Can I Know if the Media is Right for Me?

I can't help you much with the first part—having a call on your life. I can pray and ask God to help, but as I said before, ultimately, that's between you and God. But what I *can* do is to help you determine to a significant extent whether television is the right method for you.

Is television right for your ministry?

The answers don't lie within the television industry as much as they do within your own ministry. The secret is discovering those answers in time to launch your ministry to the level it needs to be.

First, there are several factors you should consider (perhaps in conversations with your key staff members or confidants):

Is Your Ministry Ready to Reach More People?

Television is a medium that allows you to reach the masses. That sounds enticing. It sounds easy. It sounds wonderfully fulfilling.

But in many ways, television is the *end* of the larger picture of reaching people with the gospel. And you can't skip from reaching a handful to reaching millions overnight. Short of dramatic, direct intervention from God, it simply doesn't work that way. On paper maybe, but in practice, no.

17

Look closely at those who are the most effective on television. They tend to have long track records. They tend to be those who have years and years of experience in preaching or teaching their message to small groups that over time, have added up to create one very large audience.

These ministers didn't just *show up* one day in TV Guide and claim a large audience share. They were out there for years doing the work *in the trenches*, finding out firsthand which portions of their messages worked and which didn't, having experiences worth sharing, and learning lessons the old-fashioned way—through hard knocks and trials.

So I ask you, have you already done everything you know to do to evangelize your neighborhood? In other words, as the scripture says, *have you already reached your Jerusalem?*

I can't tell you the number of churches that have asked me to consult with them in building a television ministry. Many call themselves *World Outreach Centers* or *International Gospel Outreach Headquarters* or something similar, but in reality they are meeting with a small congregation in a rented shopping center space, barely paying their bills.

There's certainly something to be said for having vision and looking ahead. But it's vitally important that you've exhausted every other possible avenue in your ministry, and are naturally building to a higher level of service.

Think of Television as a "Greater Reach," not Just as an "Outreach"

If you believe your ministry is ready to take the television step, I encourage you to state why you believe this to be true. What criteria are you holding up as your reasons? What proof do you have? Can you state why you are ready for a television ministry in simple, direct terms?

I challenge you to do so:

1) Why is television the next logical step for your ministry?

2) Why do you need television at all?

Is it because your sanctuary is overflowing and you need a closed-circuit system in order to send a video signal of the service to overflow auditoriums?

Do you want to take your Sunday morning service into the community in order to boost attendance at your services? Is you purpose evangelistic?

Do you have so many people clamoring to come to your church that you desire to take your Sunday morning service to the region?

Are your crusades booked well into the next few years?

Do you have a message or calling that is uniquely visual—one that could only be presented with the power of television or film?

Perhaps the key question to ask yourself is this:

Who is asking for your program?

In other words, who desires, wants, or needs more of what you have to give? Who is asking to hear you more or see you more? Why? What do they want? Is television the best way to fill their request?

It is critical that you know who your program is reaching. Who is your audience? What can you say about them? (You can only say about them what you already know to be true from your previous exposure to them, and their exposure to you. You can't simply carve out an intended audience description and hope you can reach those people.)

Again, I challenge you to state succinctly your reasons for needing to satisfy the needs of a particular group of people and why.

Are You Willing to Take the Time to Have Your Staff Adequately Trained and Prepared for the Challenges of Television?

TV producers aren't made overnight. Crews are rarely assembled instantly. Recently I had a conversation with the pastor of a major church whose television program was based on his Sunday morning church services. He wanted to professionally update the look of his program and had just purchased several hundred thousand dollars of the finest equipment to meet that goal. But after producing his first program he came to me in desperation. I looked at his show and sure enough, it was pitiful.

I asked, *"Would you go out and buy the finest typewriter, give it to an usher, and expect him to write a bestseller?"* Of course not. And just because you spend large sums of money on television equipment doesn't mean that you'll automatically begin producing high-quality programs.

Training your staff and crew is of the utmost importance. The differences in skills and techniques required is especially great between *local* and *national* programs. The expense of producing a local television show is relatively slight compared to that of a national broadcast.

Ask yourself:

Who am I willing to train for the job?

To what extent am I willing to invest in my own preparation?

Should I bring someone in from the outside who can train or update my crew?

Media Consultants

One of the most important steps you should consider is hiring an experienced, qualified, media consultant to help you make your first steps into the medium. A good media consultant or television producer can save you hundreds of thousands of dollars in mistakes, and save you years of wasted time. There are many places to find a good consultant and I've listed some references like the National Religious Broadcasters organization at the end of this book. But perhaps the easiest way is to call a media ministry you admire and get their advice. Don't be afraid to ask questions and find out anyone they recommend, and especially people with which they've personally worked.

Above all, don't be afraid to seriously evaluate a consultant to make sure he can live up to his or her reputation. What programs have they produced? What ministries have they worked with? They should be able to provide you with many program samples, references, and other information about their experience and track record.

The best consultants don't come for free. But remember—this could easily be the best investment you'll ever make in your media ministry. Considering the valuable advice and consultation they can give you, their fees are small in comparison. Don't evaluate a potential consultant by their fees; evaluate them by their track record. If they've done work you admire, or feel is the type of production you'd like to do, then they just might be the right consultant for you.

One of the greatest mistakes ministries make is to spend a great deal of money purchasing airtime, but spending very little on the production of the program. But what's the point of being seen everywhere, if the quality of your program is poor? Any consultant worth his or her salt will tell you that it's absolutely critical that you have a high-quality program before you go on the air. Remember—it's better to start locally or on one station with a great program, than to go regionally or nationally with a mediocre one. Once you establish a reputation as a ministry who produces a bad quality program, it's hard to change that perception.

Finally, give a consultant the necessary time to make your media ministry work. I've known far too many ministries that become impatient after a few months and terminate their relationship with a consultant. It takes many months and even years before you'll begin to see the fruit of your television preparation. You can't find an audience overnight, and you can't transform the level of your program overnight.

Allow your consultant and production staff the time it takes to move your program to the level it needs to be, and the results will be much more dramatic.

Training

How much time and money am I willing to invest in training myself and my team?

Before you feel completely frustrated and give up in defeat, I must tell you that one of the purposes of this book is to help you answer those questions. Study them now, and after you've finished this book come back and finish or update your answers.

Now we've faced the big three. If you have:

1) An undisputed calling,

2) An unquenchable desire to use television,

3) And a commitment to acquire the best skills and information you can find,

Then a television ministry may well be in your future.

Chapter Two

Determining Your Resources

"Do your best to present yourself to God as one approved, a workman who does not need to be ashamed and who correctly handles the word of truth."

2 Timothy 2:15

"The question for each man to settle is not what he would do if he had means, time, influence and educational advantages, but what he will do with the things he has."

Hamilton Wright Mabie

As we begin this journey, I need to make two things perfectly clear:

1.   These are the practical, real-life tools, techniques, and tips that have helped me and others develop effective television ministries for numerous churches and other ministry organizations.   Every situation is a little different, and therefore, different producers would deal with each situation in different ways. As you build your media ministry, don't worry that other producers or media consultants might disagree with some of these recommendations. Any creative endeavor will have a multitude of possibilities and options.

I've designed this workbook to help you get your media ministry up and running as an efficient and effective outreach within the budget and other constraints you deal with every day.

2.   Television is not a gender-related business. Some of the finest producers and other production staff members I have ever worked with are women, and I strongly encourage women to get involved in media ministry outreaches. Throughout this book I will refer to many roles as "he", but please understand that it refers to both men and women.

The first practical step in beginning a television ministry is *determining what resources you need, and what resources you already have.* Let's examine a few of these needs, especially in light of what you may already have.

What About a Studio?

The simplest approach to *where to produce your program* is to do it in your own church sanctuary. This is especially so if you are planning to tape your Sunday morning service as the basis of your program (either all or part of it). This usually isn't a bad idea. And it is usually inexpensive, since you don't have to build a studio or construct sets.

However, you'll still need to take a close, objective look at your sanctuary, and more than likely, you will need to make some modifications. Usually, I find that those who want to use their church sanctuaries as a set have to add television lighting and often redesign the sound system. However, that is only a small expenditure compared to the construction of an entirely separate studio. With today's new camera technology, you'll find cameras are able to shoot in lower light and under more unusual conditions than they could have in the past.

Also, as of this writing, audiences tend to like the grittier, on-location feel of programs, and they will often give you leeway in camera-related errors if they know you are live or on location.

On the other hand, you may prefer to produce your programs in a location other than your present church sanctuary.

Your first choice may be an existing building, perhaps another auditorium. But again, I suggest that you look objectively at the location to determine whether the place is suitable for television. What you may think is a nice environment or building is not always the same as a good TV studio.

Most outdoor locations have abundant problems—weather, crowd control, access to electrical power, noise, and so forth. I don't recommend them for novice program producers unless, of course, an event that you want to cover already happens to be an outdoor event. If so, I recommend you seek the advice of producers and crews who have extensive experience in shooting outdoor events. Their advice can be invaluable.

If you decide to look for a suitable studio, I suggest that you check out the studios of local film and television producers, or local television stations. In most medium to large cities, you'll find a number of local production companies that produce TV commercials, industrial and educational films, and sporting events. Realize going in the front door, however, that these companies are generally not Christian organizations and they may not be as sensitive to your ministry or your purposes as you would like.

Theoretically, a television or film production company should be able to produce a program on any given subject, including spiritual matters. Professional actors, for instance, may be asked to sell ketchup one day and medical care the next, projecting total sincerity for each type of product.

It is not unusual for a television crew to produce programs on subjects as diverse as food, automobiles, sports, and religion. Perhaps the most obvious reason is money, but it is also a chance for the production company to obtain a greater range of experience, which helps when it comes to your program. I enjoy working with these types of crews because many have such a deep pool of knowledge and fresh creativity. However, a Christian television program is vastly different from the products and concepts that most television production companies deal with on a regular basis.

It is, therefore, very important that you are absolutely sold on that independent production company's ability to be sensitive to you and to your ministry needs. If you have the slightest doubt, *shake the dust off your feet* and do not use that crew, equipment, or studios.

Early in my career, I was working with a major evangelistic crusade that was being shot by a local, secular crew in a major city. Everything was fine, until the altar call. When the evangelist asked

27

people to come forward for salvation, the non-Christian crew had no idea what it was all about. They had never seen anything like this, and rather than perform their duties, they were completely dumbfounded and startled. A couple of crew members got so caught up in this new experience that they simply stopped working and started watching (one in disbelief, and the other in total confusion).

The result? A great deal of video that was totally unusable, and ultimately, a very expensive mistake. Certainly you would want to lead these people to Christ, but at the moment, they needed to be doing their jobs. Otherwise, that experience for potentially millions of people watching on television is ruined.

Therefore, when searching for a studio production company, take the time to explain to them your particular ministry. In many cases, they will know of Christian freelancers in the community and can bring them in to work with you.

At the very least, get the professional assurances from them that your ministry will be treated with respect and sensitivity. After all, you're paying the bills.

In some cities, there will be a Christian television station in the area. Although some Christian stations have very poor facilities, many are capable of producing excellent quality programs, so my first step would be to locate a Christian station and find out if they can help. As a Christian organization, they understand what you're trying to accomplish, and will be much more sensitive to your vision as well as your budget.

What About a Crew?

Many television ministries today have spent a great deal of money and effort training their own people—or hand picking Christian companies or outsiders who understand the goals and purposes of the ministry. Don't underestimate the value of having such a crew backing you up, and in reality, standing in front of you. The personal persuasion of a cameraman may not seem important to you now, but wait until you are preaching and pouring your heart out to a camera, and you suddenly realize that the cameraman is looking at you as if you are a raving lunatic. I've seen members of the behind-the-scenes crews laughing nearly uncontrollably at a person who is ministering on camera.

That isn't the kind of support you need.

There's a great difference in having a crew that is sensitive to your goals, and knows when to remain absolutely quiet, how to deal with the audience, and most importantly of all, how to encourage the speaker, singer or host.

A few years ago, I was asked to hold a week-long television seminar at a large church outside the United States, not so much to analyze their equipment and facilities as to train their church members and staff for crew positions.

They had been shooting their Sunday morning service for some time on an amateur basis, mainly so it could be shown to overflow crowds in another room. Then the government-controlled television station unexpectedly offered them one hour a week for a program that would showcase their church and present the gospel.

They already had some equipment and used their sanctuary for a studio, but they had never worked under the pressure of producing a weekly program.

The first thing I did upon arriving was to ask them to take a long hard look at the members of their own congregation. *Who was musically talented? Who could speak on camera? Who had the organizational skills to bring a staff together?*

We then took a group of about 30 members of the congregation, all of whom had expressed a desire to work in television (but had no experience whatsoever). We divided them into three groups and started producing practice television programs. Although they had no formal training in camerawork, sound, and so forth, they were eager to learn *on the job* and very quickly, they were creating some respectable program segments. Furthermore, they improved daily, and the results were rewarding.

But I quickly discovered that the pastor already had strong ideas on who had talent and who didn't. True—he had known these people for years. But in this respect, he had no knowledge of what was required for television. One girl in particular was discouraged from coming because she had not worked in any other outreach at the church, but from the start I noticed that she had a very discerning eye. Although the pastor discouraged me, I trained her as a camera person, and discovered she really had a knack for the job.

Years later, I met the pastor on a flight from Indianapolis to Atlanta, and he brought me up to date on the progress of his television program. Not only is the program now the most watched religious program in his country, but the young girl I had trained, who had no previous experience with a camera, was now the number one camera operator in her entire country, holding a high-paying position at the government television network. In fact, the pastor said that the main newspaper in his country had just done a major feature story on her success, and she was becoming an example of how women of the country can now enjoy success in what used to be a "man's world."

I reflected later on that experience and decided that a major reason for the success of the training was the decision to *give everyone a chance.* I had not arrived with any preconceived ideas about a person's talent, or lack of it. I simply took the people who were there, and who were interested.

There's a lot to be said for motivation! It can lead a person to the acquisition of skills. The converse is not true—good skills don't necessarily result in motivation. Another young person, whom the pastor had warned me had a poor attitude, actually turned out to be an excellent director! He had just never found his niche in the ministry.

So be open to surprises within your own ministry or congregation. Just because a person doesn't do anything as part of the regular church service doesn't mean the person has no talent.

Remember, Fred Astaire's original Hollywood screen test in 1933 read:

"Can't sing, slightly balding, also can dance."

Not very impressive.

The Hollywood stories are legendary about people, networks, and studios who never recognized talent when they saw it. A young

31

George Lucas almost never made his movie *Star Wars* because the studios were sure no one wanted to see another science fiction film. Not only was it successful, but it transformed how movies were produced, marketed, and merchandised. *Home Alone* was passed over by many studio executives because they felt sure a kid film would flop. Today, *Home Alone* is one of the highest grossing films in history.

You may have talent within your congregation or ministry right now. How can you find it?

First, begin by simply finding out who is interested in television. Just open it up to all who are interested, no strings attached. Then begin their training either through a school program or a consultant/producer you can bring in (we'll discuss these options in a later chapter), and see what they can do. You'll be surprised what talents may emerge.

Of course, you'll always find staff members or church members who should not be a part of a television crew, or part of the talent used in a program. We all know those who are part of the church choir, but shouldn't be. Bless their hearts, they couldn't hit a correct note with a hammer. But they are always the people who are never late for practice, always enthusiastic, and have a great spirit. Perhaps you can get by with having them sing during a live church service, but on a television program, forget it.

Always bear in mind that one of the great rules of television, brutal as it may sound, is that the viewers out there in "television land" are simply not on your side. They have lots of programming choices— especially today when 500-channel cable systems are reality. Your objective is to keep them tuned in, and don't give them any reason to change the channel. Live churchgoing audiences are much more resilient and accommodating—they're stuck in the pew!

What About a Live Audience?

Most ministers want an audience as part of their programs. Especially for those who have little experience speaking to a television camera, it's important to have that audience support. Even with the more experienced, an audience is an important part of most successful programs, while certainly not required.

I've seen an enthusiastic congregation make a dull minister look dynamic. I've seen a minister deliver a sermon without an audience, and then show 100 percent improvement in the delivery of his message once an audience is surrounding him. And I've seen audience cutaway shots turn a fairly routine program into a program that is heartwarming and powerful.

In my younger and more naive days, I had a few heated discussions with a major evangelist who wanted an audience sitting as close to him as possible when he preached. He left me with virtually no room for television cameras to maneuver. Furthermore, the audience tended to disrupt the overall design of the set. The location of the front row of seats became something of a subtle tug of war between us.

Until one day in Minneapolis.

I was videotaping his crusade, and not a seat was empty in the 10,000 seat civic auditorium. As the prayer service began at the close of the meeting, I had a camera in the middle of a wheelchair-and-invalid

33

section. The evangelist began to ask the audience to reach out their hands to those in wheelchairs and he emphasized the part that the audience could play in building the faith of those who were sick. Suddenly, it was as if a wave of electricity went through that crowd of people. The evangelist turned to those around us in wheelchairs and walkers and said, "If all you can do is move a finger, move it. If all you can do is move a toe, move it. Start moving something!"

As I looked in the middle of that section of invalids, I could literally feel the faith of those people rise up as if there were no tomorrow. They began moving their arms, their legs, they shouted and praised God, and the audience began to celebrate with them. It was freezing outside, but inside the warmth was overflowing from heart to heart. We shot some of the best video footage I have ever produced. Because the audience was close, because the audience was alive and involved, and because the audience was encouraged to participate.

I never again argued with that evangelist over audience placement.

Whether praying for the sick is part of your theology or not, isn't the issue. The issue in this instance is *effectiveness.*

In those days, most directors kept the camera at a distance from the people. Most audience shots were wide at best, and shot from the rear of the auditorium (behind the heads of the people). The few close-ups were from distant, stationary cameras. I began to go right into the thick of things with a hand-held camera, especially during praise and worship, prayer time, or even during the sermon. There's nothing like capturing an extreme close-up of a tear rolling down someone's face to express a deep emotion. A smile, a sparkle in someone's eyes at just the right moment can sometimes do more to change a viewer's heart than a thousand words spoken from the pulpit.

It was radical stuff then, but now those same techniques are being used by every professional television ministry in the country.

When an audience is supportive, enthusiastic, and spiritually attuned to those who are on stage—those who speak, sing, and pray do their jobs better. (Plus, the crew's job is easier and usually done more creatively as well).

Also, when an involved audience is shown on camera, it lends authority to what the pastor or evangelist is doing and saying. Viewers at home have someone with whom they can relate. You'll find increased support for your message, and usually your projects.

Take good care of your audience, especially if it's your church congregation. They need to know where you are going with television, what your goals are, how to support you in prayer, and how much you appreciate their role in your television presentation. You can't duplicate the power they can bring to a program.

What About Money?

Money is certainly a key resource in considering whether or not your ministry is capable of producing a television program. In fact, it's such a serious consideration, we'll deal more directly with finances later in this book. But let it suffice for now to restate a point we've already made:

Television is expensive,

Network television is <u>very</u> expensive,

Daily television is <u>extremely</u> expensive,

Many people begin with just enough equipment to start putting their Sunday morning services on a small local cable station. Even so, you can count on a minimum investment of between $30,000 and $100,000 if you are purchasing equipment. (And that doesn't include any labor or crew to operate it.)

Finances are a brick wall to many a would-be television ministry. Money, however, is a resource that you cannot do without.

In sum, your initial key resource needs are:

1) **A studio** - *Or a place to produce the program.*

2) **A crew** - *The people who shoot and edit your program.*

3) **An audience** - *This is certainly an option, but I find a good audience is helpful for a television novice.*

4) **Money** - *The financing to get your program on the air and to keep it on the air.*

With these, you can begin to consider *format*, which gives rise to set and talent needs. Of course, once you have a program, you'll need *airtime,* or what we call *media buying.*

But first, let's first consider Who's Who in the world of television production.

Chapter Three

Producers & Directors

"The Lord has sought out a man after his own heart and appointed him leader of his people."

1 Samuel 13:14

"I'm going to get out of this film business. It's too much for me. I'll never catch on. It's too fast. I can't tell what I'm doing or what anybody wants me to do."

Charlie Chaplin

There are going to be lots of days when you'll probably feel exactly as Charlie Chaplin felt in his first few days of film work. I encourage you to hang in there. He did, and changed the direction of the film industry.

One of the most confusing aspects of television is trying to figure out exactly what people do in this business. This chapter covers *producers and directors*—the leaders of any television program.

Producers

The role of the producer is one of the least understood jobs in the business, to a great extent because the position of producer is defined a little bit differently in every production company.

37

In most cases, there are three types of producers:

1. **A financial producer**, whose expertise is raising the money and making the deals with the studio, investors, or network to get the project made. In many cases, these producers never show up on the set, but are instrumental in getting the project made.

2. **A line producer**, whose expertise is in making the movie or television program happen. This producer understands scheduling, production, crews, and has a great contact list. He knows the intimate details of every aspect of production and supervises the project through the complete cycle.

3. **A creative producer**, whose expertise is in cultivating the creative aspects of the program. This producer often works closely with the writer, director, and sometimes actors in helping guide the project through the creative process.

In television, the most powerful producers today are the "writer-producers" who are the creative force behind a program. These producers usually create situation comedies and episodic dramas, and often began their careers as writers, and then moved up to being producers.

In the first situation, particularly in independent production companies and studios (and especially the type that produce most motion pictures), the financial producer is the money *man*. Either he has been approached by a writer or director to help raise money for a program or film, or he has his own idea and is raising the money to see that idea turned into reality.

In these situations the producer pulls the strings. And why not? He has raised money for the project and it is his responsibility to see it through.

Sometimes, this type of producer has little or no production experience. He can be a businessman, or a financial expert, whose actual *hands-on* television experience is limited.

In the second case, the line producer has had extensive production experience and a background in the television or film industry. In these cases, he is doubly valuable to a project. Not only does he bring the money, he brings some experience and, hopefully, talent. It also means he is significant both on the set and to the outcome of the project.

This line producer is often more like a shepherd, overseeing the complete process of production and is often the most knowledgeable person on the day-to-day questions of creating a TV program or film.

With the creative producer, he not only has a substantial hand in controlling the budget, but many times he is an *idea man* who developed the original concept for the program and is there to see it through to completion. He will have a more obvious hand in the day-to-day work of creating the program, and will often work side-by-side with the director.

Often these three types of producers coexist. The money man in these cases is generally the *executive producer*. He controls the budget and has the final say in the chain of decision making. The *line producer* works with and for the *executive producer* in helping stay within budget and in turning the storyline into a visually exciting program or film. And the *creative producer* can be a combination of the above, a writer-producer "hyphenate," or have an individual producer credit.

There are a myriad of other combinations in the *executive producer/producer* relationship. There is the *producer/production manager*, who is actually on the set every day making sure everything happens on time and on budget. There is, of course, the *assistant producer* (self-explanatory), and then the illusive *associate producer*. I've found that most often in television, the associate producer is usually the producer's girlfriend or boyfriend or brother-in-law. It's often called a *bought credit*, because many times someone like a writer will negotiate that title into his contract in order to give him a greater credit for career advancement. We often joke that an *associate producer* gets the title because he's the only person who will associate with the producer.

It's also a good credit to give someone who has contributed something special to a program but isn't a normal member of the regular crew. (For instance, someone who made a large financial gift to make the program possible).

In the production of motion pictures, the director is often the final authority on the set, but in television, the writer-producer is often the final arbiter or decision-maker.

How Does This Relate To Ministries?

Generally speaking, the head of the ministry (who is usually also responsible for raising the funds used in the ministry), is most often the *executive producer* of a television project. If that is you, I suggest that you find yourself a good *line producer* to work alongside you to do the actual day-to-day producing.

In addition to your producer having some sense of how to handle money, good writing skills, good thinking and decision-making skills, and an ability to work with people, you'll need to find a man or woman who is spiritually aware of your ministry goals, purposes, message, and methods. I also believe that it's important that the producer personally agrees with your message, and is in relative spiritual harmony with your ministry.

He or she is your key person in developing the remainder of your television crew, so they will probably select like-minded people.

In most cases, your producer will need to have a close relationship with you. It should be someone with whom you can communicate easily, freely and honestly. It should be someone capable of turning your vision into practical reality. It should be someone who will bounce ideas back to you and not be a *yes* man.

Now if you are the ministry or church head—pastor, evangelist, or teacher—you may choose to have someone in the title role of executive producer other than yourself for purposes of communication and budget control (especially if you do not personally consider yourself to be a hands-on budget person). But in the long run, *you* are the

41

executive producer in function if not in title. You are responsible for providing the money that television eats up. You are the one responsible for the success of the format you choose. You are responsible for the level of skill of the staff you hire and the professional tone of the programs you create.

A number of ministers say to me, "I have a close confidant that I would like to put into this position, but he (or she) has absolutely no experience in television. Should he be made the producer?"

This is a dilemma, and unfortunately, I have often seen it resolved in the worst possible ways.

If you make this untrained person your producer, he or she suddenly has a tremendous responsibility for creating a television program, hiring a qualified staff, and renting or purchasing thousands of dollars (even hundreds of thousands of dollars) worth of equipment they know nothing about.

I've actually had these individuals come to me in tears because they felt overwhelmed after being put into a position that they knew little or nothing about. They loved the pastor and wanted to help, but knew they would be little more than an obstacle to an effective, functioning television department.

The fact is, a wrong decision about staff, about format, or about equipment, can cost you your program, or at minimum, waste an incredible amount of money.

On the other hand, if you are just beginning and do not already have a trained staff from which to promote someone to the position, you are likely to hire an outsider who has very little feel for your ministry, message, or capacities.

I generally suggest this:

Bring in an experienced professional as a producer on a *temporary* basis. Let everyone know—*especially the person you hire*—that you regard the position as temporary and that you are eventually going to be looking for someone within the ranks of your ministry to rise to this spot. This period might be six months or even six years, just as long as you're moving toward a target date.

You'll find a number of very talented Christian producers and consultants available to help in this manner. They are not the least bit interested in staying with your ministry for the rest of their career, but they understand your goals and purposes and would love to step in and train your staff for a period of time.

This will give your person the time to train under an expert, to guard your personal ministry interests along the way, and to learn the ropes without a waste of money, time, or the loss of morale.

Note, however, that there is a great danger in bringing in such a producer and not telling your staff and the producer exactly what you are doing. For one thing, you'll find hurt feelings all around. Your staff will have built a certain level of loyalty to the producer with whom they have shared moments of agony and accomplishment, and they will feel resentment when the person is suddenly replaced.

Should you replace your producer with a key aide while the show is enjoying great success, it is not unlike changing quarterbacks in the middle of a championship game. If your crew isn't ready for that change, it can throw your entire production staff, and thus your entire program, into a tailspin.

Consider, too, that most of your staff will already have a sense of what's going on. A motive of this type is hard to hide, and eventually your staff will feel resentment that they have not been trusted with your true intentions.

The most important thing is to keep it fair to everyone.

What Should You Look for in Hiring a Producer?

Here are some suggested don'ts:

Don't choose someone as a producer simply because they are supposedly a financial expert. Money is only one important part of the producer's role.

Don't choose someone on the basis of their having had some experience in theater or dramatic productions in the past. The two media—theater and television—are very different.

Don't hire someone who studied TV and film in college but has no practical work experience. What you learn in a classroom and what you learn under the pressure of a real production are two very different things. And although I always encourage people to pursue a college education, a recent graduate is probably not the best choice as a producer.

I take the risk of ruffling some feathers when I suggest the next item, but it is absolutely essential and will be the best advice I can give.

Don't choose someone just because they are a family member. You may be limiting the success of your program more than you will ever know. Their concern for you does not make them a qualified professional. I do suggest that you give interested relatives a chance to learn about the job to see if they are truly interested in it, and have a talent for the medium. If so, they may well become a good producer in time. And often very quickly, because the motivation should be already there.

But don't make the critical mistake of putting a family member in charge of your television ministry if they are not completely ready for the job. Your television crew is not as naive as you think, and they know exactly what you're doing. There's no way that family member will win the respect and confidence of your crew—and that will reflect on the quality of your program.

I sat in the office of a young man who had been put in charge of his family's television program just on the basis of his being an *in-law*. With tears in his eyes he related how much he despised it—he knew the crew didn't respect him, he knew his severe limitations in the field, and he knew under his leadership the quality of the program had plummeted. But he felt such pressure to continue, and he was too weak to walk away.

Today, that program is off the air, and most people who know the situation would point to the lack of a capable producer.

Beware of the "Expert"

Don't be snowed by a self-promoting *expert* either. During the past decade and a half, I've had the opportunity to work with some brilliant production people in the field of Christian television. Some have actually been some of the most humble, soft-spoken people I have ever encountered. At the same time, I've also met some real jerks masquerading as Christian TV producers.

Beware of people who talk on and on about their *Hollywood experience*. Being a successful secular program producer is wonderful, but it's not a guarantee that they can produce a successful ministry program. Besides, most people who have significant Hollywood experience don't push it or even talk about it (at least not until asked), and if they were truly good at what they supposedly did in Hollywood, they would probably still be working there!

So how do you know if you have found a good consultant/producer?

Ask to see the programs a would-be producer has produced or directed and if possible, look for their name among the credits at the end of the show. (Although many ministry programs don't use credits.)

Get references—and check them out.

Ask him or her about their doubts as well as about their goals for your television program. A true professional will be straightforward with you and willing to express their doubts as well as their dreams.

Look for honest answers here. Don't think that just because the person expresses doubts in your ideas, that he or she can't *catch the vision*. Those may be the kind of doubts and healthy criticism you need.

Evaluate for yourself how well your would-be producer communicates. Have them meet other members of your staff. Sit in on some of the discussions. Bear in mind that this person will represent you to your crew, to your equipment vendors, and sometimes to your media buyers, television stations and broadcast outlets. Make sure he or she is the representative that you and your ministry or church want him or her to be.

A producer can make or break your program—never forget that.

Sadly, I have seen this happen again and again. Several years ago, I was asked to advise a minister who was truly standing on the brink of having a large regional television ministry. This ministry had a producer who readily boasted of his track record in the business. Behind the scenes, however, it was very obvious that the producer had no personal regard for the minister. I also discovered he didn't have nearly the credits that he claimed, and that he was rapidly becoming an alcoholic.

My recommendation was to fire the producer and put together a creative team that would support what the ministry was doing. After all, television is expensive, and every minute of indecision costs. However, when the minister discovered the truth about his producer, rather than terminate his relationship, the minister sought to rehabilitate him and keep him in his position during the process. While I admired his desire to do so for personal reasons, I also recognized that he wasted several months of precious time and money struggling to produce a television program with a divided crew. Finally, after about six months of struggle, the minister eventually abandoned the television ministry altogether.

The producer, needless to say, also went out of business.

The producer role is a critical position, and I suggest that you put most of your effort into getting the right person for this job. Mistakes here will come back to haunt you for years to come.

The Director

"The fact is that a director, from the moment a phone call gets him out of bed in the morning ("Rain today. What scene do you want to shoot?") until he escapes into the dark at the end of shooting to face, alone, the next day's problems, is called upon to answer an unrelenting string of questions, to make decision after decision. That's what a director is, the man with the answers."

Film director Elia Kazan

The director, in many ways, is the heartbeat of your program. His or her talent and skill in television—as well as his or her personality—will have an indelible effect on the final program.

In the simplest terms, the director calls the shots—in more ways than one.

Television is pictures, *moving* pictures. In the early days of the movies, a film was always called a *motion picture*. Whether you call them movies or motion pictures, both names emphasize the *moving* aspect of the medium.

"The reportage of a news item in a newspaper will never have the impact of a moving picture."

Film director Alfred Hitchcock

Although the technology and much of the theory is different—the essence of movies and television is the same.

What is television?

Pictures that *move*.

Comedies in *motion*.

News programs with *movement*.

This is not the place for a critical comparison between the differing theories of television and film technique. There are many differences between the two, but one of their great similarities is *motion*.

I emphasize this point because too often ministers think they want to do a television program by sitting at a desk and talking to the camera for half an hour.

Think *movement*.

You need to be *in motion*, to be animated in your voice, face, and physical motions on the set. Those around you need to be in motion as well.

The motion needs to be quickly paced at times, slower at others. But always *motion*.

The director's role is to make your program move. The way he or she stages the sermon, the music, the interview segments, or the way he sets up the camera shots, transitions, and the tempo for camera changes are all ways in which the director moves your show to keep it interesting and exciting for the viewer.

In many religious television programs, the executive producer often ties the director's hands because on camera he or she prefers to sit or stand a certain way, look a certain way, and wants a very methodical, predictable look to the segments being shot.

If you find yourself taking over the director's reins, I'd like to make a suggestion: sit on the other side of the camera for awhile. You'll find that the director can see things that you never thought about while you were preaching, teaching, or singing.

In most situations, the director is likely to be the most artistically-minded person on the crew. It is remarkable what a talented director can do in even the most awkward circumstances, and many directors love to rise to a challenge. You'll want to look for a director who has the ability to fly by the seat of his pants—someone who can think quickly, make decisions, come up with creative solutions, and get the most out of the least.

A director with those qualities can save you money!

For one ministry, I used to cover evangelistic meetings with just one camera, primarily for budget reasons. Many times my crew would arrive in a city with just a little over an hour before the service, barely enough time to set up. We had to learn to examine the situation quickly, look for unique camera angles, and make rapid decisions about how to get the most out of the service with only one camera. In the later TV program, the meetings appeared to have been covered with two or three cameras. That couldn't have happened without a director who was capable of assessing a situation rapidly, creatively, and with an eye toward the final product.

Later, when we were able to use multiple camera productions (often with as many as six to eight cameras), we found this same ability to lay out angles and setups to be both cost—and time-saving. I literally was able to save my clients thousands of dollars a year in building and equipment rental time, not to mention overtime for the crew.

In many instances, your director does not need to have executive authority within your overall organization. He needs to answer to your producer and to you, and he needs to be a team player within the organization.

But when the production begins, the director needs to be the boss, the chief, the big cheese. You are spending money by the minute, decisions need to be made, and debates are not necessary. Behind the scenes of the program, one person must be making decisions and making them quickly. That person is the director. There can be no question about this. Your director may be linked by headset (electronically) to as many as twenty or thirty people: cameramen, sound and video technicians, technical director, stage manager, videotape operators, assistant directors, lighting directors, music director, graphics people and others—and they're all taking their cues and instructions from him.

Particularly in a *live* program, the director needs to be the answer man and he or she needs to be able to come up with the right answer within seconds.

This isn't necessarily the way sports and news programs are handled. In those complex cases, as many as three producers simultaneously may be playing important roles in the actual production of the program. But in most cases of *ministry* television, the crew isn't as experienced, the style is very different, the set up is simpler, and the goals and objectives are certainly distinct.

What happens if you don't let a director have this authority?

Once I witnessed the taping of a Christian program in which the producer decided to second-guess every decision the director was making during the program. In spite of the fact that in the middle of taping, the control room can resemble Grand Central Station—with the director literally up to his neck calling shots and giving directions—the producer stood over the director's shoulder and almost continually pointed out changes, disagreed with decisions, and gave contradictory orders to crew members.

The result?

Number one, the crew lost its confidence.

Because the director allowed the producer to exert this kind of authority, the director looked weak and unsure of himself. As his confidence eroded, the crew became less sure of its purpose, disoriented as to who they should try to please, and began to make very fundamental mistakes.

Number two, the producer and director obviously had a different type of program look in mind. One was pulling one way, the other was pulling in a different direction. The end product was a disaster.

Don't let it happen. If you are the producer, find a director you can trust and get out of the way once the program taping starts. If you are the executive producer, make certain that your producer stays clear of the action once tape starts rolling.

Now don't think that a producer should pack up and leave town during a production. Quite the contrary, during the shooting stage of a production, a producer is critically needed. He or she is overseeing the budget, supervising the crew, tracking the schedule, and making sure the resources are available to accomplish the goal.

It is very important, in my opinion, that a producer and a director for a program or a project get along well personally. Adversarial relationships can be disastrous. And don't believe that just because you are in the ministry and your staff members are Christians that these relationships will be automatic. They won't be. A good producer-director relationship must be made to happen in most cases.

If you sense that your producer and director are in disagreement, I suggest that you meet with them together and make certain that they each understand the limitations of their authority and the ground rules for the overall work they are doing. The producer needs to have final authority over the program and lay the groundwork as far as finances, equipment, and overhead are concerned. The director needs to have authority over the shooting and editing of the programs. If they have disagreements (and creative people almost always do—don't expect a disagreement-free working relationship), then make certain that they know you want them to work out those disagreements in private either before or after a program, but *never* during a critical shooting or editing session.

And realize again that every producer/director combination calls for a different set of rules. Some producers and directors work best when they don't communicate during the shoot, others work better constantly debating, and others work seamlessly as if one unit. Understand that the end result is more important than how they work— as long as it's constructive and helpful to you. If you're comfortable, and the crew is comfortable, then it's probably the best relationship for your situation.

You must also have a director who is confident. Not boastful. Not arrogant. But confident. A crew will fall apart under a director who is weak and wavering. (I know a Christian television personality right now who actually prides himself in hiring directors he can control and intimidate—and his program suffers for it).

On the other hand, your crew will not respond (at least for very long) to a director who acts like a dictator, constantly shouting orders. I once watched the taping of a live program in Hollywood in which the cameramen actually took off their headsets during a critical musical number because the director was ranting and raving in the control room to the extent that they couldn't concentrate on their work. They simply began shooting on their own, totally unaware of what he wanted or what the other cameramen were doing.

Sadly, there are a few Christian directors around the country who are known as "screamers." Certainly things will get tense during complex productions, but I have little respect for directors who scream, intimidate, or fly out of control.

I have found that a fairly loose atmosphere on the set works best in most ministry situations. Crew, pastors, and musicians can't afford to be uptight, or they will come across looking unnatural and stiff, and that is hardly an appealing subliminal message to associate with the gospel. I trust you as a minister to enjoy your work. (If there's no enjoyment—either in a sense of peace, purpose, joy, future hope, or fulfillment in life—why bother?) Always bear in mind that if you preach a message of hope, you can't keep your crew and cast terrified.

"What I look for in a director, is vision. The quality of a scene is different if it's set in a phone booth or in an ice house and the director has got to know when he wants one or the other. Scenes are different when the camera sits still or if it's running on a train. All these things are indigenous to the form."

Actor Jack Nicholson

How to Find the Right Producer and Director

In many ways, your search for a good producer or director is like the search for a family physician or attorney. You can't tell their reputation from the Yellow Pages in the phone book. Usually you need to rely on word-of-mouth. Recommendations are very important.

Once again, we return to the importance of a good media consultant. Any consultant worth his or her salt will have a phone book of good producers and directors, or have the right people on his staff.

In other cases, if you know someone who presently has a television ministry, ask him or his producer for references of people they know who may be interested.

If your budget is low, Christian universities across the country are presently training young people in Christian broadcasting. You may be able to find someone from their ranks to train—or better yet, a lead on an alumnus who has more experience and can take over a leadership role.

Once you have found someone who seems promising for your organization *(or preferably, several people)*, ask for a demo tape.

A *demo*, or *demonstration video or DVD*, is the resume for a producer or director, especially a director. Many prospective crew members—such as writers, cameramen, sound and video engineers— have demo tapes, but these are especially critical in evaluating a producer or director.

A demo is a videotape, usually in a convenient format like a VHS cassette or a DVD, that has highlights of a producer or director's latest work. In television, talk is cheap. Extravagant claims by some people are an everyday fact of life. But the buck stops at the demo.

No matter what a producer or director says about himself, or how smoothly he talks or how flashy he looks, the proof is in that little piece of videotape. (Unfortunately, I occasionally see a demo where producers or directors take credit for productions I know they didn't do. Therefore, don't be afraid to ask for supporting information, credits, or references to support the fact that it's actually their work).

Look for these two things in evaluating a demo tape:

1) Look for variety. Any commercials? Should be. You'll have products or projects to promote and an understanding of commercial and promotional techniques would be helpful.

Any documentary footage? Especially helpful in showcasing mission efforts, new building projects, or other documentary style features.

Any music? Preaching? Those are likely to be a significant part of your ministry programs.

2) Look for quality and creativity. Are the segments well-paced?

Are the camera angles innovative without being obtrusive or distracting?

Has the director kept the shows moving in tempo, or do they lag?

Does the overall production value of the segments indicate that he's worked in high-quality, professional situations?

Has the talent (speakers, singers, and so forth) been put in unusual settings or given a different look in some way?

Do the performers seem relaxed? (That's a good indicator of the ability of the director to create a relaxed atmosphere of enjoyment on the set.)

Perhaps more than anything else, look for *a sense of authority* in the segments. It's a difficult quality to define, but chances are, you'll know it visually when you see it. You don't have to be an expert to like something or to be impressed by it. You'll be able to tell by the lighting used, the set design, the performance or acting (if any), the camerawork, and just the overall feel of the program segments as to whether this is good stuff.

I'm reminded of a wonderful quote regarding this type of authority from the great writing teacher John Gardner in his book *On Becoming A Novelist.* Although he was talking here about a writer's mastery of his craft, I think it applies to most artistic endeavors, including the production of television programs:

> *"So by the nature of the novelist's artistic process, success comes rarely. The worst result of this is that the novelist has a hard time achieving what I've called "authority," by which I do not mean confidence—the habit of believing one can do whatever one's art requires—but, rather, something visible on the page, or audible in the author's voice, an impression we get, and immediately trust, that this is a man who knows what he's doing—the same impression we get from great paintings or musical compositions."*
>
> —John Gardner

You will also want to look especially for those things that should be incorporated into your own show. For example, if you plan to build a program primarily around music, and your prospective director has only shot interview shows, you may be in trouble. Perhaps you want to do a lot of on-location work. Look for examples of that. Try to find those points where this person's talents are linked to your goals.

If you are planning to do a *live* show, then you will want to see a demo tape of something that the director has done live. There's a big difference in the ability to shoot and edit a show in a normal studio setting, and the ability to call the shots while the action is actually happening.

Again remember, these are not hard and fast rules. Just because a director has limited experience in one area doesn't mean that he can't perform in others. Also, you might find the director who wants to break into a new and different type of production. As long as he's a capable, experienced director, he might be willing to work at a less expensive rate in exchange for the opportunity.

The demo itself need not be particularly well put together with transitions, and so forth. Look for the quality of individual segments on the tape.

In fact, I am immediately skeptical of a demo tape that is *too polished*. Most busy, working directors don't have the free time to spend working on their demos. You'll even find that the best directors often will just show you a compilation of their most current programs. After all, if they are busy, their best work is constantly evolving.

We should also point out the difference between a *good* segment and an *effective* segment.

Good and *effective* are not always the same. You no doubt have seen the endless parade of commercials that sell everything from vegetable slicers and dicers, carving knives, bamboo steamers, country music album collections, miracle window washers, and so forth. Needless to say, few of these commercials have ever won an award for quality. Many of them are poorly made and cheaply produced.

On the other hand, these commercials sell products very successfully. This category of advertising is called "direct response"— which means that the viewer is encouraged to respond immediately and directly, even while he is watching the commercial, usually by means of a toll-free number. And these commercials often do work very well. They may not be terribly professional, but they use techniques that are effective.

Although in fairness, that industry is growing, and today, more and more direct response commercials and "infomercials" are becoming some of the most expensive, well-produced programs on television.

For all practical purposes, the results of this kind of approach are exactly what many ministries seek or want. They want the viewer to respond either for salvation, financial or prayer support, books and tapes, or other aspects of ministry, by picking up the phone and calling the number on the screen. Or picking up a pen and writing a letter, perhaps enclosing a check.

This is not the place to argue about the philosophical role that direct response advertising techniques can or cannot play in ministry programs. But if you do want to explore this, you should find a director or media consultant who understands these marketing techniques.

Ask your potential director or producer about direct response work and the overall effectiveness of the shows he has done, the commercials he has on the demo, and so on.

The converse is also true—the most beautifully produced program may well be a flop—perhaps because of the time it aired or the message preached. And in many cases, a flop is partly the director's responsibility. He should have been comfortable enough with the minister featured and sensitive enough to both the message and the viewing audience, as well as bold enough to speak his mind to the minister and make the necessary changes.

On the other hand, a fairly low-budget, poorly done program (from a purely technical standpoint) may have met a particular need in the viewing audience and the response may be overwhelmingly positive.

In summation, I would strongly hesitate to consider a producer or director who does not have a demo tape. That means they either haven't taken the time to make one (which means they probably don't really want the job) or they don't have the goods to show (which means they are inexperienced or not talented).

Now if you are interviewing someone straight out of college for a crew position, it is likely that they either won't have a demo tape, or it won't have a great deal of variety. Look for what they do have. It may be a college project, or something they have done on their own. Look for their initiative in putting something together for you.

I remember meeting a young director who now has the responsibility for production of the promotional programs of a major computer game manufacturer. Years before he had approached them right out of college with a poorly produced video on their product which he had made with his own money and his dad's home video camera.

The video presentation looked terrible technically, but the corporate executives could see that the young man had an unusually strong understanding of the company and their computer games. Based on that feeling, they offered him the job, and he's turned out to be a great success.

So *watching* and *evaluating* a demo tape are two different things. I suggest that you view a demo tape in private (or perhaps with one or two close associates)—but without the person who made the demo tape present.

And if you feel completely inadequate, contact a producer you trust at another Christian ministry and ask for their evaluation of the tape. Their thoughts and criticism may be helpful as well. The small amount of money you pay for their time and evaluation may over the long haul, save you tens or eventually hundreds of thousands of dollars from hiring the wrong director.

Finally, after you have narrowed your choice, by means of resumes and demo tapes, you will want to interview your prospective candidates.

See if you are able to communicate freely with them. See how they fit in with others on your staff. Look for their ability to communicate quickly, but not flippantly. Look for their willingness to discuss their weaknesses as well as their strengths. Talk about ideas a little. See if they have creativity to contribute.

Remember—talented producers and especially directors are often a creative lot, which reflects in their clothes, personal habits, and mannerisms. Don't automatically rule out someone because he or she isn't exactly like everyone else at the church or ministry office. Give them a little creative space and you will often be amply rewarded.

On the other hand, make sure they can deliver when they step up to the plate.

And when in doubt, hire the person only for a specified contract period. It may be six weeks, or thirteen shows, or one pilot program.

See how the person operates on the job before you commit yourself to a staff position and salary.

Production Companies

You will generally find two types of producers in today's marketplace.

One is the *individual producer*. *Individual* as in *one* person. He or she is usually a freelancer who works solo.

The other is the *production company*—a *team* that can do everything from produce your specific program to negotiate time on local stations or cable outlets and, in some instances, even do the advertising and promotional work associated with your project.

They each have their strengths and drawbacks.

Individual Producers:

These men and women are often chosen because:

—They are cheaper to hire than an entire team.

—You may already have a good support team within your ministry such as artists and graphics assistants, set builders, promotional experts, financial advisors, and so on. All you lack is a leader.

—They are specialists. They devote all their time
to one particular task—getting you a top-notch product.

The Production Group:

These companies offer complete turnkey operations. They are usually hired because the person, church, or ministry entity has few resources or they are looking for better, outside talent. They have the capacity to analyze your position and provide everything you need to get the project off the ground and into the airwaves.

The drawback? *They can be expensive.*

I suggest that you do give them an opportunity to present what they can do for you. (They may list some things that you hadn't even thought of). And overall, their price may not be any more than what it will cost you by going out and shopping for many different individuals.

Today, "outsourcing" is a popular philosophy among business professionals. Outsourcing simply means going outside your organization to handle projects that you're not capable of doing well. Why spend the money hiring more staff, training them, purchasing equipment, paying for insurance, benefits, and more, when the task can be outsourced to a more qualified company? When the task is not part of their core business, secular companies are outsourcing in record numbers and finding fantastic results.

I also see more and more Christian churches, ministries, and organizations doing the same. If you don't have a strong graphics or art department, TV department, media buyers, or anything else, I encourage you to investigate the possibility of outsourcing to a more qualified and capable company. Even if it costs a little more, most people feel that it's more than worth it in saving liability, space, staff, and headaches.

> If you do outsource, make certain they are:
> 1) *Tuned to your vision and goals.*
> 2) *An experienced, reputable organization.*
> 3) *Up front about the total fees and costs.*

Some work on a straight fee, others on a retainer plus costs, and still others take a straight percentage of the budget. This is an area where mistakes can be costly and expensive, so be careful and get good advice.

The Remainder Of The Crew

Except in certain situations, hiring the rest of the crew shouldn't really be your concern as the executive producer. Your primary goal is to find a producer and director with whom you can work. It's up to the producer and director to find technical experts, cameramen, set designers, artists, and so forth. The producer is considered the captain of the team, and he needs to have the leeway to put together the team with whom he can work. It's up to the producer to juggle budgets and set up schedules. He'll also need to have the clerical assistants he needs.

Just for the record, virtually all television-related professionals do have demo tapes or portfolios. If you wish to take a more hands-on approach to the entire crew selection, your best input is likely to be in viewing these demos with your producer and director.

If that's what you decide to do, here are a couple of thoughts to keep in mind.

Look For Professionalism And Creativity

Professionalism and creativity are the key attributes to look for in any crew member you hire. Their skills in a particular field are a given. Without those skills, you shouldn't be considering them in the first place. The problem is, many ministries don't go beyond evaluating skills.

Professionalism and creativity are the benchmarks I set every prospective crew member against. Creativity does not mean letting a crew member do his own thing. You need to provide boundaries.

Imagine sending a child out into the front yard to play ball. In the front yard there are no fences, no boundaries, and nothing to keep him from wandering out into the streets or perhaps into the ditch next to the road.

At first, the kid will love having no boundaries, but you'll find yourself constantly shouting, "Watch for the cars, and don't fall into the ditch and break your leg." As your child plays, your constant concern and nagging will make him likely to be so nervous about looking out for the cars and not falling into the ditch, he'll probably have no fun.

Now put that same child in the backyard where there is a fence and everything is limited and tell him to have fun, and he probably will have a wonderful time! Why? Because there's nothing for him to worry about within the fixed boundaries. He can do anything he wants because he's safe within those boundaries.

Creative energy within a ministry setting often needs to be channeled. But within those boundaries you need to leave room for fun. A relaxed crew is going to give you a better product; I am firmly convinced of it.

At the same time, professionalism must be present at all times.

I have produced television programming across the United States, South America, the Middle East, Africa, Russia, Europe, and the Caribbean. Never once have my crews failed to bring back what they were sent out to produce. And each time, the entire crew had a great time, even in the most difficult of circumstances. The reason? We choose to do things in a professional way.

In this context, another word for *professional* is *disciplined*.

Professionals are disciplined people. They know when to have fun, when to pull out all creative stops, and when they must burn the midnight oil to bring home the bacon.

I have one particular cameraman and engineer that I enjoy traveling with very much, not only because he has a good sense of humor and knows how to relax, but because he does his homework, knows his equipment, and triple-checks everything.

A number of years ago, I was in the nation of Swaziland on a shoot with the Swazi Royal family. The humidity was so high that it shut down our videotape machine and we lost our ability to record. The moisture in the air was triggering a built-in internal mechanism that stopped the recorder in order to keep it from being damaged.

Fortunately, I had an engineer who was able to analyze the situation in the field and come to the conclusion that the moisture was enough to trigger the mechanism but not really enough to damage the recorder or the finished product. He stayed up most of the night, and with very few tools, rigged a system for bypassing the shut-down switch and rewired the machine to record normally.

I felt like Captain Kirk watching Scotty bypass a critical engineering system to save the starship Enterprise.

My engineer basically saved what would have otherwise been a ruined and very expensive trip. (Not to mention the potential embarrassment in front of the royal family of Swaziland).

Professionals Know Their Equipment and Know How to Use It

On one of my first trips overseas, I was with three engineers in the Middle East. As we arrived in Tel Aviv, we discovered that the two large crates with our TV equipment had been quarantined for three days. This was during one of the first waves of bomb scares that hit Israel in the middle 1970's and the officials had adopted a policy of pushing aside every crate for three days, for fear it would explode. There was nothing we could do but wait.

At the end of the three days we retrieved the crates, and feeling already behind schedule, we discovered in horror that the Israeli customs officers in New York City had taken the crates apart to examine the equipment before it even left the United States. They had taken the cameras apart, unscrewed the lens, taken out the circuit boards, and dissected the videotape machine. And then they had tossed all the pieces back in to the crates, nailed them shut, and sent them on.

After we recovered from our initial shock, we took the equipment to our hotel room and began to piece everything back together. We worked most of the night and by morning everything was in good working order. Lesser engineers would have thrown up their hands and purchased a ticket back to the United States.

Professionals Get the Job Done, No Matter What it Takes

You'll want to surround yourself with those who know the discipline of television, not just the glamour, fun, or excitement of it.

Chapter Four

Choosing A Format

"With many similar parables Jesus spoke the word to them, as much as they could understand. He did not say anything to them without using a parable."

Mark 4:33, 34

"The Lord's Prayer has 56 words;
Lincoln's Gettysberg Address has 266;
the Declaration of Independence has 300;
but a government order on cabbage prices
contained 26,911 words."

William Windall

Several years ago, I was asked by an internationally known evangelist to accompany him to Nigeria, in order to record his crusades on videotape and produce a documentary program about the trip. A few weeks before we were scheduled to leave, the committee of sponsoring pastors in Nigeria called and asked that we prepare a commercial for use on the government-owned television stations in order to promote the crusade services.

I immediately assembled footage taken from previous African trips, added a stirring musical score, and wrote a script including all of the pertinent information about who the evangelist was, the locations and times of the meetings, and of course, the invitation to *come!*

I arranged for a professional narrator to come to the studio and record the script. For its intended purpose, it was an excellent commercial. The evangelist approved it wholeheartedly and we sent it to the committee of sponsoring pastors in Nigeria for use on television.

Weeks later, upon actually arriving in Nigeria, I was immediately pulled aside at the airport by the pastor's committee. They explained that the commercial I had sent them was *terrible* and that it would need to be re-done before it could be used. Embarrassed and a little confused, I hurriedly went down a mental checklist trying to figure out what I had possibly done wrong. The official language of Nigeria is English—no problem there. The camera angles or persons shown? No problem. Music? No problem. Graphics? No problem.

Then a car pulled up and I was instructed to go with the driver to the studio to meet a Nigerian pastor who was waiting for us there to redo the commercial. Driving through the narrow streets of Lagos, Nigeria, at top speed, I wasn't sure if I was traveling with pastors or government agents. When we arrived at the studio, I met a young man who seemed to be about 25 years old. He introduced himself and said that he would like to change the script. At that point, I was willing to do whatever they asked, so we set up the cameras, framed the shot, told the sound man to be ready, and cued the pastor.

I wasn't quite prepared for what happened next.

This man immediately began waving his arms and legs up and down frantically, and at the top of his voice he shouted:

"CCCRRRUUUSSSAAADDDEEE!"
"CCCRRRUUUSSSAAADDDEEE!"
"CCCRRRUUUSSSAAADDDEEE!"

He then burst out in a torrent of shouting, giving the times and places of the crusade meetings, all the while flailing madly with his arms and legs, and literally screaming at the top of his voice. At every chance he could get to take a breath, he would interject the long screeching shout of

"CCCCCRRRRRUUUUUSSSSSAAAAADDDDDEEEEE!"

I sat stunned.

He finished, walked over to me, put his hand on my shoulder and said, "Now *that's* the way to make a television commercial."

There was nothing I could do. The pastor's committee broadcast the commercial just as that young pastor had done it. I was horrified, but my hands were tied—the pastor's committee loved it. Not only did it air on the national TV station, but they also took the soundtrack of the commercial and played it from speakers mounted on the tops of vans that drove through villages and remote regions of the countryside.

For the next three days, I couldn't escape the ghostly screaming voice of the pastor shouting, *"Crusade!"* In the market, the streets, the villages—it seemed like it was played from every speaker in the region.

I was sure my commercial—and possibly my career—had been ruined. These people weren't professionals—I was. With a commercial like this, I knew it would only be a matter of time before the entire crusade was a failure, and my services would be terminated.

Finally, at the opening night of the crusade, I arrived at the polo field (where the meeting was scheduled) in fear and trepidation. Would anyone be there? The evangelist would hold me responsible if the crusade was a flop, and I was waiting for the hammer to drop.

But as I stepped out of the car, I looked out over an incredible sea of faces. They had come from the cities, the villages, the forests, the plains—and I suspect to this day that some of them must have appeared just out of the woodwork. At least 30,000 people were gathered there. They stretched out into the blackness of the night as far as I could see.

The only way these people could possibly have learned about the crusade was through that commercial which then triggered word-of-mouth advertising.

I learned a very valuable lesson that night that I have never forgotten:

It takes different approaches to reach different people.

The Importance of Selecting the Right Format

Every audience needs its own format. You no doubt have seen the classic Hollywood scene featuring a beret-clad movie director screaming, *"ACTION!"* at the top of his lungs, only to shout, *"CUT!"* later. The word *action* is used to start, and *cut* to stop. In the context of an entire program, *format* is the structure of what happens in between.

You may opt for any number of formats, and several formats may be mixed together to form even more variations on the basic themes. What follows is a discussion of several of the major formats used in Christian television today:

- ***The Interview Format***
- ***The Music Format***
- ***The Preaching or Teaching Format***
- ***The Variety Format***
- ***The Drama Format***
- ***The Documentary Format***

We'll look at each in turn and then deal with some specific questions and answers.

The Interview Format

This is a program format largely made up of a host who interviews guests. You've seen it a million times on both secular and Christian television programs.

Its strengths are:

—*It is simple to produce and direct.*

—*It is inexpensive.*

—*It takes little setup time.(No elaborate lighting, no elaborate set, no complicated sound required.)*

Most Christian television programs today have at least a portion of their programs devoted to the interview format. (It may, however, be an interview format with an implied host—such as a testimonial that is rolled into the program as a feature segment. You may never see the interviewer on the tape, but the answers to the questions are provided by the guest and are usually given in what is considered to be a basic interview format.)

This is also a good technique to use for conveying information about an event, product, or project.

Its weaknesses are:

—*The interviewer.*

—*The interviewee.*

In case that sounds over-simplified, let me explain. An interview format can be a dynamite choice with the right person doing the interviews. But if the person has a difficult time handling the guest or the subject matter, you may be in for a nightmare.

Also, not all ministers are good interviewers. An interviewer must be a good listener. He or she must be genuinely interested in what the person has to say, be alert at all times to what the person has just said, and be able to keep the interview moving (in pace), asking the right questions and providing the right comments to keep the interviewee on track and to the point. He must do his homework, which means doing whatever it takes to know enough about the person being interviewed to ask the unusual questions and bring up the unusual tidbit of information.

Many pastors, teachers and evangelists are good interviewees. They love to talk and answer questions. But many just aren't good listeners. They tend to overpower their guests with their own charisma or sense of *presence*.

They may simply be bad listeners.

Natural ego plays an important role here as well. I once directed an interview program with a host who never let his guests talk. As soon as the host would ask a question, he would answer it himself! We would come to the end of the program, and the guest would barely have introduced himself.

By contrast, experienced interviewers like Charlie Rose or Larry King give their guests plenty of time to answer questions.

You will find that the camera angles for an interview format are fairly predictable. There is the two-shot, sometimes the lateral—or side-shot—often of the entire set, the close-up of the interviewer, the close-up of the interviewee, and the occasional audience reaction shot. You will also need a director who can keep the visual pace moving, even when the interview is lagging.

As for the interviewee, he or she may have a story to sell, or information to give that is interesting or vital, but I would suggest that they must also be personally vibrant. They must be visually animated (in voice, face, and physical movements). They must exude genuineness about themselves and their message. They must be able to communicate their message in an interesting way. They must be self-motivated, yet able to take direction.

The interview format is an excellent choice for programs that choose to deal with controversial subjects (such as abortion, prophecy, morality, politics, and so forth), since the more conflicting opinions, the more interesting the program.

During programs that deal with these controversial issues, the purpose of an interview program is to create dialogue. If you want to preach about a subject, we'll look at that format later. But if you decide to produce an *interview* program, make it exactly that—let people speak. Their differing points of view are what make the interview format a success.

One interesting note to consider is that during secular infomercials, my experience and research indicates that phone calls spike up during testimonies. Apparently, a program host can talk all he wants to about a product, but when the viewer actually sees someone like him or her using the product with great success, it really makes an impression.

Testimonies trigger response.

I believe the same holds true for ministry programming. A pastor, evangelist or teacher can talk on and on about a subject, but when the viewer sees a powerfully compelling testimony of someone whose life has been dramatically changed because of that teaching, it really makes an impression.

Therefore, use testimonies. Begin now finding people in your church or ministry who have experienced fascinating encounters with God, and begin shooting those testimonies. People love to hear other people's stories, and it can have a fantastic impact on the success of your program.

The Music Format

Those of us who grew up in the South no doubt remember the *"Gospel Singing Jubilee."* This program was a pioneer program in Christian broadcasting using the music format. Sometimes using a host only to tie together the loose ends before and after songs sung by outstanding guests or by regulars can result in an entertaining and moving format.

Virtually all Christian television programs have some element of music in them. Music adds variety. It adds interest. It provides a good bridge from one mood to another, from one guest to another, from one segment of the show to another.

Pastors, teachers, and evangelists will also tell you that nothing sets the stage for ministry like the right song.

But music may also become a format in and of itself. Music videos are causing a number of Christian entertainers to consider musically formatted programs even as I write this manuscript, and we now have 24-hour-a-day Christian music channels featuring professionally produced music videos that proclaim the gospel.

Here are some suggestions about music as it may relate to your program format:

1) What works in church doesn't necessarily work on television. In fact, it often doesn't work. Always keep in mind that your television audience has already been exposed to some of the finest Gospel artists in the country. Thanks to Christian radio, concerts, and other television programs, they've heard good quality music, presented with high quality production techniques and are pretty sophisticated in their listening habits.

The bad news is, standing Bessie May and her husband Ralph in front of a camera while they sing a duet of *"Shall We Gather at the River"* is probably not going to be very palatable to the public (unless you are seeking to provide them with comic relief).

Please don't misunderstand my intent here. I'm sure Bessie May and Ralph are sincere, genuine, and wonderful people. But you can never forget that your job on television is to attract as many people to the Gospel as possible. You can't give them any excuse whatsoever to change that channel if you want to keep them long enough to present the gospel message.

My own personal experience over the years indicates that a typical viewer will give you an average of 2-5 seconds to decide to watch your program. In a 500-channel universe, it may even be less. If you've ever sat on the sofa with a remote in your hand, you know I'm right. That's why it's so important to eliminate any distractions or reason for them to change that channel. I often tell my clients that today, your message isn't the most important thing. Production values are far more important. Because if you can't keep the viewer watching long enough to hear your message, you've failed.

Therefore, never stop examining your program for anything that distracts, distorts, or gives the audience a reason to watch something else.

The good news is, in many situations, local churches have enormous talent just waiting to be discovered.

Take an inventory of your own people. Perhaps you have a music director or minister of music who can help you. Find those you believe can musically support an effort in television and begin their training. Share with them the burden your organization is about to undertake. Impress upon them the need to train—seriously and literally—for this task, just as you are training yourself for a role in television.

Some of them may drop out right away. Don't be discouraged. Concentrate on the ones God has given you.

Should You Seek Outside Musical Talent?

I suggest you wait until your program format is fully established before you do this—at least on a regular basis. First, you don't want to make serious, and sometimes expensive, commitments until you are sure of the direction of your program. This may take several weeks (and sometimes months) after you have started broadcasting. This is especially true if you have plans to hire a large band, orchestra, or singing group.

Second, you will often find outstanding talent within your own congregation, and it never hurts your credibility to show that you are supporting and developing your own congregation and the families within your own ministry. Whatever successes come out of your own ministry help legitimize that ministry to the public.

Third, booking talent can be expensive. Should you go this route, make sure you research the background of the talent before you invite them to be on your program. Don't just seek a big name for the name's sake. If you have the opportunity, read their books, listen to their recordings, and especially, watch them on other Christian television programs.

Fourth, you'll have to pay for permission to use their songs on your program. This gets into copyright—which many pastors think means "your right to copy." This is not a big problem, but you need to know that when you use songs on your program, there are royalty and publishing fees that need to be paid. I'll deal with this later in the chapter, and a good producer or media consultant can guide you in making these decisions.

And most importantly, ask a friend. I strongly recommend that you get references from others in the ministry who may have had them sing at their church, at a crusade service, or better yet, on their television program.

Perhaps one of the greatest sources of talent is singers and musicians right on the verge of success. They're not famous enough to be priced out of your range, they need the exposure, and they're very talented to boot. In order to find this select group, you need to work closely with the music community in your area and stay abreast of their always changing careers.

How Do You Pay Musicians?

Artists can be paid for their work in a number of ways. One of the most common is the *love gift* or honorarium. This is a gift either based on an offering taken during the performance, or on a standard scale that you have set for a particular program. For a regular program, this is a good way to go because it usually does not involve a great deal of money.

Also, remember that if the singer or musician has just released a new recording, they can greatly benefit from the publicity your program is bringing them—especially if you let them mention the recording on the air. Therefore, in many cases, you can get the artists at no charge, since they need that publicity to sell records.

Another tip is to constantly keep in touch with the speakers and musicians that are touring in your area. If you know that a famous or popular singer will be at a local church on a Sunday night, perhaps they would consider staying over and shooting an episode of your program on Monday morning. That saves you any travel expenses for the talent, and they might be willing to do it at a reduced rate or at no charge since they're already in town. Of course these things should be set-up in advance, not at the last minute.

I've even taken a camera backstage at a local arena for a short interview with major performers before or after they went on-stage for a show. If it's approved ahead of time with both the artist's manager and the building manager, that can be an exciting and very inexpensive way to have major guests for a minor cost.

Other musicians—generally the top-rated ones—flatly refuse to deal or negotiate. They will rarely accept anything less than the fee they've set. (Others may attempt to charge you more than they would normally charge for a concert engagement in your church once they realize that television is involved.) I suggest that you stick to what you can afford, and if you cannot negotiate a figure that you are happy with, move on to someone else. You are probably better off staying with those who appreciate the television exposure and will work with you.

Don't worry about how to find musicians and guests. Once your program begins to show signs of success, these musicians and singers will begin to come from everywhere. (And thank God for them.)

You may also want to explore the opportunity to scout out and feature musicians at local Christian schools and universities, other churches, and even crusade meetings held in your area. You'll probably be surprised at the amount of talent within a 50 mile radius of your home base.

If you are interested in the top Christian artists in the country, an excellent resource is the *Christian Music Networking Guide* from the Gospel Music Association (1205 Division St., Nashville, TN 37203 Phone - 615-242-0303 or on the web at "info@gospelmusic.org".) Refer to it for contact with artists, managers, and agents.

Agents and managers, by the way, are the ones you usually go through in hiring this kind of talent. Don't let these people intimidate you. They may sound like big shots at times, but believe me, they want your business. There are many wonderful people in this industry, and most will do whatever they can to help you and will deal fairly and honestly along the way.

If others seem difficult to work with—and as a normal business practice you should always be on guard—move on. There are always others around the corner.

As a note of caution in all of these discussions, I recommend that when dealing with an artist through a manager, booking agent, or promoter of any kind, you should work with an experienced attorney. Always confirm things on paper, and get experienced professional advice if you have any questions.

What About Music Rights?

The majority of the songs you will feature on your program were written by somebody who makes his living writing music. Songs are copyrighted in the same way that books, movies, and other creative endeavors are—primarily because they are *properties* subject to theft. A copyright is a legal right to determine who else may publish or profit by the use of your creative work. It is basically an ownership statement.

In a practical way, this means that every time you plan to use a piece of music on your program, you will need to find out who owns it, and pay them for using it. To do otherwise is technically and legally stealing their property. The official term is using it without expressed permission.

The payments that are made to musicians and songwriters are called *royalties*.

As programs grow in popularity and begin to be regional and national in their scope, you definitely need to pay close attention to music rights. How do you go about it? Look at the bottom of a piece of sheet music or the inside jacket of a tape or CD. You'll usually find the name of the writer, arranger, and publisher. Call the publisher and ask about the rights for the type of program you are doing.

If in doubt about what you should do regarding music rights, ask. Start with your local Christian or secular television station. They can answer many or all of your questions related to music rights. A number of unions, guilds, and associations are there to answer just such questions. Or ask any experienced musician. There are also a number of companies that can specifically help you take care of the business aspects of "clearing" music that appears on your programs.

These companies charge a fee, but in many cases their experience and efficiency make them truly cost effective in terms of man-hours to your own organization. (Remember outsourcing?)

Also, there is a category called *Public Domain*. This is the category creative work enters when the copyright has expired. That releases you from any payments for the music, since the music is now cleared and in the *public domain*. Many hymns and other older pieces of music are in this category, but it's best not to guess. Once again, get professional advice from your local television station, a music clearance company, a publishing company, or an organization like BMI or EMI Music Publishing. Today, the Internet is a fantastic source of information on copyright, music rights, royalties, and clearances.

What About Music Libraries?

These are audio tape or CD libraries that feature original background music for use on programs, commercials, teaching tapes, and so forth. They can be an excellent and relatively inexpensive source of music. The music is usually high quality, and is much cheaper than bringing in an orchestra, hiring a composer, or recording a custom arrangement.

You can pay for the library either on a *yearly payment* basis, on a *drop* (per use) charge, or a *buyout*. The term *drop* was coined during the days of record albums when every *needle drop* (or dropping the needle on an album cut) meant a different song selection.

Especially during the early stages of your media ministry, I strongly recommend you explore *buy out* music. This is music that you pay for when you purchase the library and you never pay again. In the age of computer and synthesized music, these libraries are excellent quality and will suit your needs just fine.

All charges such as copyrights, production charges, composer fees and more are usually included in these library fees.

I strongly recommend that you purchase a music library or a combination of different libraries. It will make a dramatic difference in the effectiveness and quality of your program.

What About Custom Musical Arrangements?

A *custom arrangement* is simply an original song or musical score created especially for your program by a composer. In the past, this was an expensive and time-consuming effort, since a composer or writer had to arrange the music, then hire an orchestra and/or singers and record the music in an elaborate studio.

Today however, with computer technology, a single person can write and record a complete orchestral soundtrack in his own home quickly and easily. This is an important alternative in producing programs today because of two reasons:

1) The music is written and recorded to perfectly match your program. (That is, the music reflects every mood, emotion, and aspect of your program.)

2) You own the music and will never have to pay royalties again.

The Preaching Format

One of my greatest challenges in Christian television is getting church and ministry leaders to understand just how unique and different the medium of television really is.

A light bulb is not a candle you plug into a wall.

A car is not a horse with wheels.

A television is not a radio with pictures.

A television program is not a church service.

See where I'm going?

Television has its own strengths and weaknesses, and those strengths and weaknesses need to be properly exploited if we are to be as effective as we possibly can.

A church service is not the most effective use of the medium, but today church services probably represent the vast majority of Christian programming. That's not to say that sermons and teaching situations shouldn't be on television, but they need to be done in a more innovative way that takes better advantage of the medium.

The preaching format is probably used most effectively by the Billy Graham Evangelistic Association. Today, the Harvest Crusades with Greg Laurie are an excellent example of shooting preaching programs from a evangelistic perspective, and the weekly program produced by Pastor Joel Osteen of Houston's Lakewood Church from a church perspective.

Greg Laurie and Joel Osteen are two of the few people who can preach, and do little else but preach, and people will still watch. That's both a testimony to their skill as preachers and the powerful anointing that's on their lives and ministries.

Take my word for it, it's very difficult to get an audience for a program that has preaching and little else—particularly a secular audience.

Ask many people about a preaching program and you will get a one word response: *boring.* The talking head approach (seeing nothing but a shot of a person's head while he or she talks) is one of the most dull and lifeless ideas in television and in the secular world. Even newscasters are rarely seen for more than a few seconds per segment these days, and even that's generally with a photograph, location, or graphic background of some type behind them.

Let's consider for a moment the difference between a *live performance* and *television*. When you attend a *live event*, such as a play in a theater, a church service, a sporting event, or a concert, part of the performance is the awareness that you are seeing real, live people do something in three dimensions at that very moment in time. It's a *hot* medium in that all your senses are engaged in the process. You watch them pace, you can hear them breathe, you can see anger and joy expressed with their entire bodies. You can feel the electricity of the crowd and the excitement of the moment.

Television is different. It is a two-dimensional medium, and it is *cold* in the sense that many of your senses are ignored by the medium. You don't have a tactile sense of the environment in which the event you are watching is happening. You don't have the smells and many of the sounds usually present in a live performance or event. At the same time, *the average viewer is usually doing something other than watching television while he watches your program.* He or she may be eating, looking through the newspaper, sewing, or getting dressed. My wife Kathleen does the ironing in front of the television. Plus, people watch your program via that little glass box on the other side of the living room, bedroom, or kitchen. The size and shape of the TV set alone limit the viewing experience.

In sum, the average viewer is not paying attention exclusively to you.

That fact alone is one of my greatest criticisms of the medium of television. In a movie theater, people sit in the dark, focusing ahead on the giant, lighted screen in front of them. They have come here exclusively to watch the movie, and everyone sits quietly (hopefully) and concentrates on the film.

I found this to be true some time ago when I saw a motion picture that I really loved and admired. Wanting my friends to see it too, I rented a copy at the video store and invited the couples over to our home.

Phil Cooke

When I put the movie in the VCR and hit the start button, my wife immediately got up to fix everyone some dessert. I looked over and my friend went to the kitchen for a cup of coffee, and his wife opened a magazine and started reading it. The other couples started talking. I was infuriated! I wanted everyone to watch and enjoy this movie like I had in the theater, but they were all doing something else!

And that's when it hit me. *That's the way people watch television.* Few people turn down the lights and concentrate exclusively on the TV program. Instead, they do any number of other activities while they supposedly watch a program.

There's another major difference. In a live event, you are virtually always preaching to a group. Crowd fever can play a big part in your own ability to deliver a message. Ironically, television brings you to the opposite end of the spectrum. Although television is actually reaching far more people that you ever could in person, the successful communicator knows that on television, you should act as if you are preaching to an audience of one person. Rarely more. Yet your sermon must be just as powerful. ✳ ✳ ✳

For all its massive reach, your presence on television should be treated just as if you've been invited into a family's living room for the evening.

How Can I Do It?

First, you must preach directly to the camera as if you are talking to just one person. During his best years on television, Oral Roberts was always a master of this technique. He had a well-developed ability to preach to the television camera as if it were a living person. His eyes register intensity, his nostrils flare, his lips are tense as he reaches out across the invisible glass barrier into your home. He is entirely focused on the viewer, not on himself. It takes a rare ability to concentrate so completely on that task that you pour yourself into just one focal point. It's a technique that must be practiced and practiced and practiced.

To begin with, you have to have that level of spiritual intensity inside you. You must have that emotional fire blazing before you can channel it to a camera. I'm not talking about a contrived performance here, but a sincere, focused, intensive delivery of your message.

Second, you must be able to confine your gestures and physical movements. You must develop an ability to *gesture with your eyes*—to do things with your head that you would normally do with your hands, to become a master of the facial expression. On stage, in a large church, or in a crusade service auditorium, your physical movements can be much more expansive, and should be. After all, they have to see you all the way to the back row.

But on television, what happens below your neckline is rarely seen if you want to have an intense one-on-one encounter with the viewer at home.

Third, your message must generally be very simple, very direct, and very short.

Although every situation is different, rarely can a preaching segment command much more than 10-20 minutes of time. (Most preachers are accustomed to taking twice that much time for a Sunday morning pulpit sermon, and many take three and four times that amount!) You'll need to be concise and to the point, and yet at the same time, provide for moments of levity and anecdotal information and stories in order to maintain interest. A short sermon is usually much more difficult to write than a long one. There's no room for rambling.

Every word must count.

Once again, experience indicates that people tune in and out of programs about every seven minutes. That means people rarely are willing to watch long, detailed sermons on television.

I recognize that most Christian programs will have a preaching segment. As I said before, preaching is a very ineffective use of television. When you have the awesome power of a television or film camera that can travel anywhere in the world, reveal dramatic presentations, powerful and anointed music, it's a shame so many Christian television programs concentrate on preaching alone, but that is another book.

How long that preaching segment lasts should be a major concern to you. It certainly will be a major concern to your director. It will be the most difficult thing to make interesting, from a visual standpoint. Although a well-shot sermon can add a great deal, it will generally be the one time when the director really can't help you add a lot of motion or diversity to retain audience interest.

I suggest you talk over your sermons with your director in advance so that the director can help you with illustration ideas. Perhaps your sermon can be done in an unusual setting. Perhaps there are props you can use that will add visual interest. Perhaps there's a portion of your sermon that can be illustrated by other visuals, or even by a videotaped story featuring a person with a testimony or an expert with added information or examples.

Don't forget the power of graphics. When I was working on my master's degree I uncovered some interesting research that revealed when graphics are used in a newscast, the audience retains more information and can remember it for longer periods of time. The study was done to encourage news directors to add more graphics to their newscasts. I think the same thing should be done on Christian programs. For instance, television preachers act as if their TV audience were sitting there with Bibles in hand. The reality is quite the opposite! More effective graphics can include scriptures, sermon points, and other key information.

Let's begin to be more creative in our use of on-screen graphics instead of just using it for a toll-free phone number.

Preaching on television is one area of the program where you will need to train, and train hard. It is my opinion that fewer than 25 percent of the television preachers on the air today truly know how to preach effectively on television. Like all physical and mental skills, it's something that takes practice and training, and then more practice and training, and so on and so on.

But it's worth it.

Practice and training in this area can make the difference between a so-so program and a truly dynamic and effective one. (Recall our earlier discussion about the difference between good and effective? It's especially true in this area!)

The Variety Format

This is one of those terms that is exactly what it says it is. It's a variety of several formats, a little of this and a little of that.

Other than drama programming, the variety format is probably the favorite for television through the years. That's because few topics and few performers are able to attract and hold our attention for longer than a few minutes at a time without working from a dramatic script of some type.

With this format, the producer and director have a good opportunity to mix it up for a change of pace that keeps the viewer asking for more. Many of the Christian family-oriented programs on the air today use the variety format for good reason; it allows them the opportunity to present a number of messages in an abundance of different styles that hold attention.

How Can You Make These Programs Unique?

1) Develop some type of angle that keeps you from being just another variety show. This is usually done by selecting an important issue or topic. Create a topic that is controversial, in the news, or on people's minds.

2) Select a strong professional host.

3) Work to make each segment strong. A variety format is only as strong as it's weakest segment. Why? Because that's the

moment the audience will change the channel, and you'll never get them back.

4) Select a different or exciting location. The setting can add a great deal to a variety program—either an in-studio set, or a great location.

5) The variety format, overall, is probably where your program will end up, even if that is not your first choice. This is simply because few interviews, few musical renditions, and few sermons are capable of occupying an entire program, especially week after week, or day after day.

The Documentary Format

The documentary format is the most specialized format for the majority of ministries today. Years ago, The Moody Institute of Science probably made the most of this format in its numerous science and documentary films that debuted during the 1950's and 1960's.

Sadly, few ministries have followed their lead. Today, the documentary format is mostly used for ministries to describe the different facets of their worldwide outreaches, intense fundraising, or the recent obsession with end-times subjects.

Although there is certainly nothing strictly wrong with these approaches, the documentary format can be a rich platform to explore historical, political, theological, scientific, and social issues.

I would urge you to consider a documentary format, if not as your main thrust, at least as a supplementary format. I would love to see more ministries produce occasional documentaries on abuse, homelessness, divorce, or other subjects. It is more complicated and time consuming to produce, but it can be a powerful format, as many award winning Christian documentaries can attest.

The Drama Format

For the purposes of this book, I won't go into detail about dramatic formats, because few churches or ministries have the experience or funding to pursue dramatic segments or projects. However—I do think it's the single most needed format in the Christian media world today. A quick survey of television reveals that the most popular formats on secular networks are situation comedies, episodic dramas, and movies—all dramatic formats. They are the most popular secular programs by far, and yet they are virtually nowhere to be found on Christian television.

As you grow and become more experienced in your media ministry, I would encourage you to explore the possibility of dramatic options. They don't have to be complete movies. They could be short segments to enhance a preaching presentation, or dramatic commercials and promotional pieces. Wherever you start, dramatic programming has enormous potential.

Frequently Asked Questions About Format

#1 - Does a typical church service make a good format for television?

Yes and no.

A church service can be translated fairly inexpensively to television. You have a built-in audience. You have a built-in studio (with some adaptations, as we mentioned earlier). Your audience may have slightly lower expectations about talent (musical and otherwise). And perhaps most positively, a church service already accommodates a variety format. In addition, if you are a pastor, it's the place where you are already delivering your best work, and is a natural transition from the pulpit to the television ministry.

Now let's consider what is probably the biggest pitfall:

You may be preaching to the wrong audience.

The most successful programs on television became successful because they reached a particular audience segment—referred to as a demographic breakdown. They captured what in the industry is called *market share.* In other words, they targeted a market, and that market found the show, realized intuitively it was just for them, and continued to watch.

Perhaps we could look at it this way. The audience out in *television land* is generally not a churchgoing audience. Let's assume for the sake of argument that the people in a church service are hopefully Christians. In that case, the purpose of a church service is to disciple

97

Christians, while giving those few who are lost an opportunity to accept Jesus, or to join the church, or both.

But the people at home are mostly just flipping channels when they come across your program—and for the most part, if they wanted a church service, they'd attend one for themselves. (After all, it's more interesting to be in an exciting church service that just to watch one on TV.)

I had a discussion on just this point with a minister a few months ago.

The church is located on one of the most beautiful resort islands in the Caribbean. The pastor of this independent church, which had experienced phenomenal growth, was convinced that the time had come to reach his entire island, and the other islands as well, through the media.

As we drove from the airport into the city, we passed countless resort hotels lining the snow-white beaches and I asked him about their outreach to the thousands of visitors that come to this island each year from around the world. On a person-to-person basis, evangelism would be nearly impossible, he told me. These visitors had come for a vacation and they were not interested in being hounded by someone preaching Jesus while they were sunning on the beach, playing tennis, or eating at one of the many fine restaurants in the area.

But he went on to say the visitors did not reject the gospel when it was presented on television. "The tourists," he said, "need to be reached with the gospel. It's as if the mission field has come to us."

And then he asked, "Should we broadcast our existing Sunday worship service or use something else?"

I asked, "Is the intended purpose of your program primarily evangelism?"

"Yes," he said. "To the tourists, and also to the unsaved people in our own nation and on other islands. The needs are so great on these islands, and only the power of Christ can help the people solve them."

Then I asked, "If you had the opportunity to preach to a large group of tourists gathered together for a crusade service, would you preach the same message you preached on Sunday morning?"

"No," he said. "My church members need deeper teaching and they love the praise and worship aspect of the service. But to a group of unsaved visitors, I would probably have music with a little different flavor, and then preach a salvation message."

I asked, "If you had your own countrymen together for an evangelistic rally, would you preach the same message and sing the same songs as you do Sunday morning?"

"No," he said. And then he added, "I think we've answered the question, haven't we? If I'm going to reach the unsaved people who live on this island and who come to this island as tourists, I'd better plan a program just for them."

Point made. Case closed.

If you attempt to use your main weekly service as your television program, eventually someone is going to feel short-changed. Either your regular church members are going to feel that they aren't being considered, and aren't being fed the "meatier spiritual food" they need, or your television audience is going to feel that you are talking over their heads and not reaching them with a message they can understand and relate to.

How did we resolve the situation in the Caribbean?

I suggested that the pastor use his Wednesday night service for television and clearly call it a "Wednesday Night Television Service." I advised him to make a concerted effort to recruit his members to come to this service as a part of their evangelistic outreach to the community, and to encourage them to pray and intercede for the viewers at home before the program began. I encouraged him to find the talent and to preach the sermons that would reach the unsaved, and to invite those on the island who were interested in knowing more to attend the following Sunday's service when there would be a special class (similar to a Sunday School class) just for those who might have questions.

This seemed to be the best of all solutions for this pastor. He could still use his own auditorium as a studio. He still had access to an audience—and even more, now an audience with a real purpose and mission—and he still had access to talent within his church. But his message was tailor-made for the local, mostly unsaved TV audience.

Many of you reading this would disagree with our approach. I realize that many pastors preach a salvation message every Sunday, other pastors present an in-depth teaching, and others take a multitude of other approaches. Some get a good response from their viewing audience, but most do not.

In a single book, I cannot begin to work out a plan for every pastor or evangelist's approach to his sermon and to his proposed television audience. Some Sunday services work very well on television, but others do not. The factors are complex and involve a pastor's personality, subject matter, delivery, and production values—not to mention spiritual issues. Every situation is a little different, but each is critically important if we are to use television in the most powerful and effective way.

The important thing to gain from this section of the book is that you should spend considerable time trying to understand who your television audience really is and how to effectively reach them. If your television audience is a church-going audience, then your normal Sunday sermon would be appropriate. If they are unsaved, then you should aim the thrust of your program in that direction.

This is still a highly controversial aspect of Christian television, and I can only give you my own personal view on the issue.

Demographic studies have been done at places like the Christian Broadcasting Network, The Barna Group, Ellison Research, and other Christian media organizations, and I suggest you seek out these studies for more information. But through my own experience in Christian television, and the experience of those I trust and admire, I've found that in most cases the existing audience for most current Christian television programs are Christians themselves.

The only programs that seem to be reaching the unsaved with any success are the programs that really focus on that issue and are willing to take a risk. They are programs that air when the unsaved are more likely to watch, and are programs that don't ask for money directly on the air because they are not reaching people who want to support it, they're reaching people in need.

Programs for both the unsaved and saved are equally valid, and that decision will come more from your own personal calling than anything else. I would like to see more of both, as long as the quality increases, and the producers seek to relate better to their audiences. Either choice would be appropriate.

This is a subject that we could talk about for years. I would call on major Christian producers, networks, and stations to support better and more accurate studies to help define who their audiences are and how to better serve their needs. You would be surprised how much money is spent in Christian television based on gut-level decisions, a reaction simply from a single direct mail offer, or an off-the-cuff comment from a friend. I know one major ministry leader who bases his programming decisions on aspects his barber likes about his program—probably not the most reliable or accurate source of media information.

The secular broadcast industry spends millions each year on research, and they make billions of dollars as a result of that information. As better research techniques are developed, the Christian media should embrace them and apply them to our industry. Ultimately, better marketing and research will be a valuable aid in understanding our potential audience and getting out the gospel message more effectively.

We will deal more with audience demographics in a later chapter.

#2 - How are a "script" and a "format" different?

There are those who firmly believe that having any type of script whatsoever for a Christian program destroys all spontaneity and eliminates the role of the Holy Spirit—and hence, no life, no infusion of the Spirit, no spiritual gifts, and no room for creativity. I fully understand that concern, and agree with it in many instances. However, I also believe that when a script is prepared in the right way and used with the right format, it can be a wonderfully liberating tool.

Every show needs some type of script. It may not need every word tightly scripted, but generally, any program host needs opening and closing lines, time frames for certain segments, suggested transitions, questions, teasers, and taglines.

Let's talk a minute about the role of the writer. I opted to include this discussion here, rather than in our discussion about producers and directors, because a writer is very often a director or producer as well. In other instances the writer for a particular segment or a particular show in a sequence may not be a permanent staff position but a task that fluctuates or is passed around among several people. In still other instances multiple writers may work together to create a particular segment or show.

"For by your words you will be acquitted, and by your words you will be condemned."

Matthew 12:37

"Words are the most powerful drug used by mankind."

Rudyard Kipling

The role of the professional scriptwriter is frequently misunderstood in Christian television. In fact, most ministry leaders have little knowledge of how a professional writer can dramatically increase the power and impact of their television programs. I am reminded of the famous quote by movie producer Irving Thalberg who had a similar view when he said: *"What's all this business about being a writer? It's just putting one word after another."*

Here's my opinion of what they should and should not do, and why:

First, a professional writer (as in a <u>good</u> writer) can make a bad program good and a good program great. How? By using an almost unlimited arsenal of ideas designed to spark the viewer's imagination and cause that viewer to be moved in new and powerful ways.

A writer does not, however, write your sermon. That's your job and your area of expertise, and if you can't do that by yourself (or at least mostly by yourself), you probably need to start your training for television in that area. Having something to say is the first step—being able to deliver it is the second.

That isn't to say a good writer isn't a valuable asset in assisting you with your sermon. He or she can help you with research, both from the Bible and from other sources, and also in developing illustrations. He or she can help you with phrasing of major points. A writer can help by providing insight and, in general, developing concepts and ideas.

I'm an unusual television producer, since I have a Ph.D. in Theology. With that background, I have written a few sermons for television preachers. I enjoy it a great deal, but I find that the most talented preachers use me more as a sounding board and a source of ideas and illustrations. It's only the weak ones that will use a sermon of mine verbatim. (In fact, I quit working with those preachers years ago—if they can't write a sermon themselves, they need to be in another line of work). But make no mistake that a talented writer can add a great deal of dramatic impact, illustration, and editing skill to an already written sermon.

A good writer is always open to spontaneity. Few scriptwriters will attempt to thwart the chemistry or energy that may emerge when two exciting guests work together, when an audience hears a moving piece of music for the first time, or when a particular truth hits home to you in an emotional way you hadn't anticipated. If anything, a good writer hopes to put certain word chemicals together in order to get a reaction. They are usually pleased when that reaction sets off even greater ones or leads to new ones.

Finally, a good writer is a great asset when the time comes for program opens, transitions, questions to ask guests, closings, commercials, and promotional segments. Who is going to prepare that information? Who is going to string those words together in an exciting way? It's likely to be a writer!

#3 - *When do you need a writer and when don't you?*

If your format dictates that all you're going to do is sit behind a desk and preach then you certainly don't need to hire a professional writer. You also probably don't need one if you are just broadcasting your church service.

You do need one if you are going to build a program around a theme—such as a sermon topic, a controversial issue, a musical medley, or a holiday.

Several years ago I worked with an evangelist who wanted to produce a special Christian program in which he related his childhood experiences. He hoped to show that even in the midst of poverty he had always enjoyed Christmas because of strong family relationships and the deep faith that his parents had in God and His Word.

The writer of that program made certain that the theme of family and faith was interwoven into every aspect of the program. The opening and title of the show reflected that idea. The transitions each reflected it. The promotions and advertisements reflected it.

As the individual links were welded together, the chain was strong and uniform. The show was a great success. The message came through loud and clear.

Holidays are not the only successful themes that a Christian program might use as a springboard. Such issues as violence, drug abuse, education, and lifestyle choices are ripe topics for programs to be produced from a Christian perspective. The task of the writer for these programs will be to make every aspect of the program work toward the whole, to keep the program focused, and to make certain that the programs have a balance of provocative questions and interesting answers.

#4 - What is the relationship between writer and director?

Usually a writer works closely with a director to create scenes, determine locations or design sets for the program. For example, a program about drug abuse might be more powerful if shot in a dirty inner-city alley than in a nice clean television studio or church sanctuary. That's likely to be the type of suggestion a writer will provide, or that a writer and director will come up with as they create together.

A good writer generally has ideas about the pacing and sequence of a program. Many Christian programs seem to be in something of a rut: opening, greeting, song, testimony, sermon, another song, wrap-up and product offer, closing remarks. But what might happen if you started the program with a dramatic testimony? Again, that's likely to be the type of idea that will come from a writer-director idea exchange.

Of all the people on your television crew or staff, the writer is likely to be the one most keenly concerned about the composition of your audience. Writers are trained to write to someone, not just to manipulate existing situations and talent. A writer, and particularly one with an advertising background, can really help a minister and a director reach out to new audiences.

The following are some of the questions a writer is likely to ask about your viewers. (If a writer doesn't ask these questions in some form or another, you certainly should ask them in your role as executive producer!)

—Are the viewers family oriented?

—Is it a multi-cultural audience?

—What is the religious background (if any) of the viewers?

—What is the average age of the viewers?

—How many viewers have children?

—How do the viewers make their living? (Blue collar, white collar, professional, independently wealthy, retired?)

—What are the viewer's values? (What means most to them in life?)

As I said earlier regarding audience demographics, it's difficult to nail down this information without using reliable research sources such as the ratings services or your local television station. These services are expensive, and with the multiplication of outlets via cable and satellite networks, it's increasingly difficult for any one service to get a true reading about total audience size or composition. But informal surveys that you do within your ministry, generally through questionnaires or focus groups, can give you a great deal of information.

A good writer will ask for demographic details. Have them and be prepared to share them and discuss them.

#5 - *How do you find a good writer?*

Experienced producers and media consultants often have established relationships with good writers, and a production company will usually have one or more writers on staff. Again, you may call on various ministries whose programs you admire and ask their advice. Sometimes staff members of one ministry are willing to moonlight to help you get off the ground, or at least are willing to refer you to someone else whom they trust and whose work they admire. Christian colleges and universities are another source.

Since you will want to experiment at first, you probably don't need a full-time staff person as a writer at the beginning of your program. (Indeed, you may never need a full-time writer at all.)

#6 - *How are writers paid?*

Freelance writers (those who work on a project-by-project basis) are generally paid by the project. In other words, they will do the script work for a flat fee, rather than work by the hour. Others work strictly by the hour.

The length of your show, and whether it is local, regional, or national, will influence the price charged.

Another variable is the amount of actual "script" that you desire. If you are only looking for some thematic ideas, a promotional commercial, and format suggestions, the cost will be less than if you are asking for a complete outline, suggestions for musical guests, questions for interviews, location ideas, and so forth. Be sure to identify up front all that you are expecting your writer to give you, and be in agreement on the cost.

Using credits on the program is a good bargaining tool in getting a lower price, especially with young or inexperienced writers. If the writer wants to work with other ministries, a credit on your program will mean a lot. That works for other positions as well. I've gotten numerous calls from clients as a result of their seeing my name on the credit list of various productions.

Be wary of those who bill themselves as *idea people*. I often meet people who attempt to convince me that they don't actually write scripts, but they have great ideas. I generally avoid those people like the plague. They quite often don't know anything about good television formatting, pacing, or sequencing of ideas. *A writer writes*—it's as simple as that. A good writer writes and rewrites and carries a project from first idea to finished reality.

Idea people - at least in my experience, usually don't actually have the skill or the discipline to complete the job. They are long on suggestions and short on follow-through and, very often, their ideas don't work in the practical realm of budgets, schedules, and existing talent and circumstances.

A good writer is worth his salt because he can start with a blank page. You'll be surrounded by people who can criticize or make changes once they actually see something already written, but the ones who can start with that blank page are the ones with the most talent and in the most demand.

A good writer will have a portfolio of work to show you, and possibly a demo tape of programs he or she has scripted.

Remember, too, that when you hire a writer, you aren't just paying for words. You're paying for pace, rhythm, background research, a theme—in other words, a complete package that holds the show together, gives it unity, and keeps it moving with interest, variety, and a sense of enjoyment.

Look for a well-executed idea that's innovative and intriguing, has well-crafted dialogue, unpredictable endings, cultural sensitivity, and one that avoids pat "Christian" phrases and terms. (Don't get me started on the overuse of "Christian lingo.")

Don't expect a writer to hit a home run every time at bat. Just as you probably write many versions of your sermon before you're happy with it, so a writer often writes many drafts of a script before it works. It's important to understand that a writer welcomes positive criticism and wants you to work with him or her during that process. The great playwright Lillian Hellman said, "Nothing you write, if you hope to be good, will ever come out as you first hoped."

Therefore, give your writer the creative latitude to explore new options and ideas, and take the risk of trying new approaches.

You are very fortunate, indeed, to find a writer with whom you are comfortable and who can really churn out the words for you. They are rare and valuable people.

#7 - *What is a storyboard?*

A storyboard is a tool used by producers and directors to visualize the finished program before it has been shot. It is a useful device in that it gives other members of the crew an insight into the visual images that are floating around in the director or producer's mind.

A storyboard may be considered a version of your program told in still frames or still pictures. Each scene is laid out by a director or artist with a still version of the main shots drawn in, and the key words of the script added under the appropriate pictures.

Storyboards are used extensively in the advertising world, where they are critical to the presentation and production of commercials. The boards are shown to clients before any footage is shot in order to get an agreement on a concept before very much money is spent. They are also helpful to give the crew an idea of how the commercial will look, and the sequence of shots.

You'll rarely have a need for a storyboard for an entire program (30 minute or 60 minute), but you will find them a useful tool in designing openings, closings, special musical numbers, commercials, and other short but important pieces.

If you're like me and aren't a very talented artist, StoryBoard Artist is a computer program that helps in creating and drawing storyboards. It is produced by PowerProduction Software of Los Gatos California and can be reached at 800-457-0383, or contacted via the World Wide Web at: www.powerproduction.com.

#8 - What happens between the time the program is taped and the time it airs?

Editing.

The process is much like that of editing a sermon or a manuscript. It's just more complex and expensive.

There are some programs that aren't edited at all. Most of these are called *live* shows and are shot to be finished programs. In this case, the viewer sees the program the moment it is produced. Certain segments of a live program are produced in advance—the opening, the closing, and other transition points, as well as any commercials or features that may be rolled into the program as special segments. The editing happens as the show progresses. What you see is what you get!

In most other cases, however, various segments of the program are shot in numerous locations and at various times. Multiple *takes* of a sermon, interview, or song may be shot. And the best of these are then the raw elements to be strung together into a completed version of the show.

A few preachers I know prefer to preach until they are finished and then have their sermons edited to fit the time slot allowed or designed.

Editing is also called *post-production* since it happens after the shooting.

During the editing process, your director works with a technical staff to pull together the segments of a show, working against the clock, in order to make certain that all segments are in proper proportion to the whole. The pacing and the sequencing of the entire show are completed as originally scripted or envisioned, so the total program has the look and feel desired.

#9 - *Where do you go for post-production work?*

Post-production equipment is expensive and you should never purchase it unless you are completely sure of your program needs and of your financial stability. In most cases, you'll want to begin by renting editing rooms from TV and cable stations or production companies that specialize in that business. This is a growing industry and you'll find outstanding facilities all across the nation, not just on the East and West Coasts. Check them out. Take your time and ask questions.

In reality, I wouldn't worry about this choice very much. The post-production facility will usually be chosen by your producer and director depending on program needs. Today, most editing systems are computer based, and we're seeing prices drop on a regular basis. These are called "non-linear" systems because the program is digitized onto a computer hard drive and the editing can take place in any sequence whatsoever. The editing systems that I've personally found to be the most reputable and reliable are Avid, Final Cut Pro, and Media 100, although there are other good choices as well. You'll find many edit systems to choose from and I highly recommend you select one that is widely used and has a long track record in the industry. Churches, ministries, and Christian TV stations often purchase less reputable systems to save money, but find that they have expensive problems in the long run.

#10 - What is the difference between "format" and the "design" of the show?

— VISUALS—

Production design is primarily concerned with the setting, the style and the atmosphere on the set. Forget the sermon for a moment; forget the music; forget the guests. Look at the set:

Is the set a living room, outdoor scene, church, classroom?

What colors and types of clothing are the speakers and musicians wearing?

What type of chair is the host sitting in? Is he or she behind a desk?

These are just a few of the many questions that concern a production designer.

The person or persons involved may be called an *art director* or a *set designer* or a *set decorator*. In multi-million dollar movies, these designations have important meaning, but in the world of your television program one person can easily cover all these areas.

The work they do is actually very important to the overall image that you are presenting. Always remember that television is a *visual medium,* and these people are concerned with the visual impact of your program.

115

Much of their work can be termed *subliminal.* The conscious mind may not perceive the cues, but the subconscious mind is always at work.

For example, a singer performing in a formal dress with sparkles and sequins conveys a much different message than one who wears a sweater and sits on a rug by a warm fire. They may be singing the same song, and both with equally fine voices, but the visual impact will be dramatically different.

In the same way, one host may wear a suit and sit behind a desk in an executive-style chair to present a sermon. Another host chooses to wear a sweater, and casually sit on the corner of that same desk.

With each approach, the visual message is quite different.

One man preaches in a pool of light with stark contrasts between light and dark. Another preaches to an audience that is close enough for him to reach out and touch them, and he stops to do so periodically in his message.

Once again, in each case, the visual impact is different.

Your director is a key element in making these decisions, but your production designer or art director can help you achieve impact, communicate, and avoid mistakes and wrong impressions.

One thing you don't want to do is to distract your viewer from the main object of the program—your message! And generally, this message is coming out of your mouth. Therefore, you want the focus of the program to be on you.

What happens if you are wearing a cheap plaid sport coat, striped shirt, polka-dot necktie and during your sermon you shake a lock of hair loose so that it falls in front of your eyes? Friend, the audience isn't likely to even hear what you are saying. They will be too busy watching *you*.

Learn how to dress. Learn what colors and styles are most flattering on camera. Throw out your plaids and floral designs.

Electrify your facial expressions, not your wardrobe.

I am not advocating that your show have the look of a bank lobby, or you dress like an accountant or attorney. Tasteful can still mean fun, festive, and stylish. I *am* advocating that you continually consider the visual impression. Does it match your message? Does it convey the mood of what you are saying? Does it express your goals and purposes in sharing the gospel?

In the old days, we always warned against wearing bright white, bold stripes, fine patterns and certain colors, mostly because the camera resolution was such that often these colors and/or patterns would take on a strange, other-worldly look. Although technology has changed a great deal from those days, there is still something to be said for most of these examples. When in doubt, I always move toward the conservative side, and advocate simplicity, style, and good taste.

Consider especially your setting for various segments of a program. A program on the resurrection should probably not be done in a funeral-home atmosphere—although a different program actually done from a real funeral home may be dynamic! A program on child abuse should probably not be done in a carnival-style set.

Today, research indicates that as much as 70-80% of the message of your program comes through the visual sense, so be acutely aware of the importance of what is seen.

The axiom is this: *your visual message should match your spoken message,* in television and in all forms of communication!

Evaluating the Finished Program

Ultimately, no one cares how well-written a script or rundown is. Nobody cares how inexpensive or expensive a program was to produce. Nobody cares how difficult a show may have been to put together. Nobody cares how hard you labored. The only thing that matters is, *did it work?*

After encountering an unusually large number of problems editing a program, one producer said it this way when I was a young assistant director: "Don't tell me about the labor pains. Just show me the baby."

But how can you tell if you've done a good job with the finished product? Perhaps we should ask, how can you tell when you've done a good *enough* job with a product? You'll always find one more item you could change, delete, something to add, to make your show just a little better. Working against a deadline, you often have to sit back, take stock of the situation, and determine if it's a good enough job and let it go.

That doesn't mean that you should settle for second-best or lower quality. It's just that in the creative process, something can always be done just a little differently and maybe just a little better. If you don't stop adding those extra touches, you'll never get a program on the air. There will always be a balance between what you wanted to do and what you were able to do, given constraints of time, money, and talent.

The best way I know to go about an analysis of your own program is to look at it piece by piece. Evaluate each portion of the show, and then look at the whole.

Here is something of a checklist to use in that process:

1) **The opening:** Does it grab attention? Is it appropriately paced? Is it interesting? If you don't capture the audience's attention within the first 15-30 seconds you may not get it at all. Does the opening tell the viewer what the program is about? Be very critical of your opening. It's the key to having the rest of your program viewed. It must not drag.

2) **The Greeting:** Is it positive and upbeat? If, of course, you want to be serious and threatening, the tone will be slightly different. Still, you will need to have a lively facial expression on the host. Is the viewer given a preview of what's in store for him or her during the remainder of the program?

3) **Music:** Do the musical selections fit the theme of the show? Are they in the same style as the rest of the show? Is it entertaining?

Does the music minister? Are the musicians skilled? Is the selection technically well-done from a musical standpoint?

4) **Sermon:** Is it powerful? How would you do it differently? Is it evident that the anointing is on this message? Were you prepared? Is the message easy to understand? Is your presentation comfortable and not tense? Is there an opportunity for audience response? If desired, have you included a prayer time that is meaningful?

5) **Guests / Interview:** Do they reflect the values of your ministry and your program theme? Are they interesting? Have they contributed positively to the overall program? Have they communicated their testimony well? Is there any point at which the interview drags?

6) **Closing:** Does it leave the viewer with a changed attitude about the subject? Have your spiritual objectives been achieved? Have you given the viewer an opportunity to respond to your ministry? Has your name and address (or phone number) been clearly displayed for a sufficient length of time?

Bear in mind that the closing of the program is the last thing the audience sees and, therefore, is one of the primary things they will remember. What is the last visual image you want to give to your viewers?

At times, your director and producer may have wrestled with a program for so long, or with so much intensity that they become too close to the program to be an accurate judge of its values. You also may be too close to your own contributions to the program that you no longer can see it as it truly is. At these times, ask others to join you in viewing a program. It may be a secretary, a clerk, or a delivery person from the warehouse. (Those people are likely to be your typical viewer anyway!) Get their opinions. Find out what they especially liked about the program.

Were there any portions of the program that they felt were weak? (Don't ask them what they didn't like since, as your employee or associate, they may not tell you out of fear or respect. Always couch your questions in terms of "what do you think we could improve?")

In some cases, especially if you are launching a brand-new format or trying an untested idea, you may want to hire a marketing firm to conduct a focus group session for you. For a fee, these companies bring in people from all walks of life, show them your program, and have them fill out a questionnaire and discuss it. This is not inexpensive, but in the long run you could save a great deal of money, and avoid the embarrassment of a major flop. But be prepared, since these people don't know you and will be completely honest and merciless. One pastor I know was so devastated upon hearing the reaction of a focus group to his program he couldn't produce anything for six months. They were right on target about the shortcomings of his program, and he knew it, but it was tough to handle. In the long run he got over it and bounced back with a far more effective program.

Occasionally you may find yourself trying to understand a finished program. In the final analysis, there's no objective means to decide whether a program will work. Sooner or later, you will have to go with that strange feeling in the pit of your stomach.

Let me emphasize, this is ultimately your decision. In the television industry you'll find a lot of armchair quarterbacks who will say "I told you so" after the results come in. Don't listen to them.

Also avoid committee evaluations. The tendency of committees is for everybody to disagree about something or somebody to disagree about everything. But you can certainly count on everybody finding at least one thing they don't like—it's the nature of criticism. You can listen to a committee to the point of confusion or distraction and still not have your mind focused on whether the program is successful.

From the viewer's point of view, your television outreach is a reflection of you, either as a church leader or as an individual leader in a parachurch ministry. The viewer sees the main speaker or host as the person leading the show. He or she doesn't place the blame on anybody else but you; conversely, when they applaud any segment of the program, that's a vote for you as the leader.

I am definitely not suggesting that you close yourself off from other people's opinions. You need them. You need to hear what others think. But in the long run, when it comes time for a final approval and a final decision, the buck stops with you.

All of which leads us to this conclusion. If there's something you aren't comfortable with in your program, take these steps:

1) Isolate exactly what it is that you don't feel right about. "I just don't like it" or "I just don't feel right about it" won't communicate with those who can fix the problem. Is it the tempo of the show? Is it what

has been said? Is it something that hasn't been communicated? Is it the music? Does your message come across as too hard, dogmatic, unfocused? Have you failed to give your viewers a challenge?

Whatever it is, try to focus and be as specific as possible about what you feel is wrong and work with your director and editor in an attempt to fix it.

2) Talk it over with your producer and director. Ask them what they suggest you do differently. No matter what happens, don't come into a meeting with your guns blazing. You will be better received if you aren't accusatory, even if you feel that they made important mistakes. Remember, they're on your side.

3) Always bring your discussions back to your original vision. If your vision is kept firmly in focus, in your own heart and in the hearts of those working by your side, you're likely to have more cooperation in fixing what isn't working.

4) Take action. Don't think the problem will be fixed by itself. Television is too expensive to delay. If you've hired the right people, your producer and director will deal with the problem quickly and effectively.

Chapter Five

Television Equipment

"And He has filled him with the Spirit of God, with skill, ability and knowledge in all kinds of crafts."

Exodus 35:31

"A determined soul will do more with a rusty monkey wrench than a loafer will accomplish with all the tools in a machine shop."

Rupert Hughes

Very often the first question that a ministry or church asks when it begins to explore the possibility of having a television outreach is, "What kind of equipment do we need?"

Wrong.

I have intentionally placed this discussion after *resources, personnel,* and *format.* It is only after you have made decisions about these other crucial elements that you should even begin to think about equipment.

If anyone tries to sell or rent equipment to you before you have answered the key questions about your goals and format, your resources, and the people you intend to work with, run from him as fast as you can!

I am often amazed at the churches and ministries who seem more interested in the public relations or bragging rights about having the most expensive, and in some cases, most *obscure* types of equipment they can find. I recall one minister who could hardly wait to show me his studio, and I was truly amazed. There was more equipment sitting there than could ever be used by that pastor (or two pastors for that matter), and I was amazed at the overkill. Furthermore, I quickly realized that he had pieces of equipment he would probably never use, while he was lacking certain items that he would desperately need should he continue to pursue the format he was considering.

I have also been called in several times to help churches after they have made the mistake of purchasing equipment before they had produced even one program. In each case, the ministers were making a format change because their first attempt at the program had been unsuccessful. In one case, the church almost went under financially because of their mistake in purchasing very expensive equipment before the program was fully launched.

I suggest you always wait until after you have produced at least your first series of programs, and have had time to measure their response and effectiveness, before you consider buying equipment.

First of all, I am not a qualified television engineer, but after spending 25 years working in television, I've learned how to make important decisions regarding equipment and who to seek for advice. And while this cannot be an exhaustive discussion about what types of equipment are best, I do suggest these five questions as a means of getting started on equipment selection. I suggest you discuss these questions with your consulting engineer or any company with which you are investigating equipment.

1) Will the program be produced mostly in a studio, or will you be spending considerable time on location?

Several years ago I went to the headwaters of the Amazon to shoot a mission team taking medical supplies deep into the jungles of Brazil. At that time, you can bet we needed very specialized equipment, and certainly not the same equipment used in a typical television studio. Although technology has enabled cameras and tape machines to be much smaller over the years, and there is an unprecedented blending of equipment uses, there are still important differences that make certain types of equipment right for a particular job. Know your needs very specifically, before you buy equipment.

2) How highly trained should studio engineers be?

Sometimes a more expensive camera—that needs far less upkeep than an inexpensive one—is your best choice if you do not have well-trained engineers available. Having full-time engineers on staff is certainly not a necessity, but you should always have access to well-trained engineers to regularly maintain your equipment, even if it is only on a contract basis.

3) What are the light levels in your sanctuary or studio?

This is an especially important question to ask if you are planning to use your church as your studio. Today's cameras can work with a great deal less light than the previous generations of cameras. Since television lighting means both *brightness* and *heat*, the right decision means more comfort for you as you preach on the stage.

A friend of mine had been asked to consult with a local Christian television station in the South because they were having a problem—they couldn't get any guests to come on the program. No one understood why, but for the longest time, they just couldn't persuade anyone to come and be on their talk show.

On a hunch, my friend went into the studio and looked around. Glancing at the overhead grid that held the lights, he asked them to turn on their normal television lighting. Taking a light meter up to the stage, he was stunned to realize there were more than 500 foot candles of light being blasted on that small interview set!

Translated, that simply means the set had become an oven.

Today, most cameras are sensitive enough so that 100-150 foot candles is more than enough light to be comfortable and deliver a good picture. In addition, there is a new generation of fluorescent lighting that is designed and color-balanced for television—lights that will keep the brightness up but the temperature down.

4) Is the equipment company you are considering a reputable one, and will it be there to solve your technical problems

and to support you as you install your equipment? Will it be available to you several years down the line?

You may pay a little more for equipment from a reputable company with a good track record of support services and quality equipment, but you are likely to be happier in the long run.

I strongly recommend that you investigate companies generally recognized as the standard of the industry. I know ministries right now who got "great buys" on equipment, but the manufacturers have since folded, and it's impossible to get service or parts.

5) What level of production is the program going to have?

Is a network-quality image required? Or are you just closed-circuit broadcasting to an adjacent auditorium? The quality of the program will determine the quality (and price) of your equipment. This is not the place to discuss the wonderful impact music videos and documentaries have had on the television industry, but today, 35mm images are mixed with Super-8 film, and high-definition video images are mixed with Hi-8 and VHS. In programs where you are using image grain, black and white, and other effects to achieve a creative "look," mixing image formats and poor quality is not a problem—it's an asset.

But in your situation, you want to start with the highest quality image you can afford, and that will be the basis of our discussion.

Rent or Purchase?

I am a strong advocate of *renting equipment*, especially during the initial stages of your program.

When I first started my career, I had the opportunity to witness an interesting comparison. I did freelance work for a small film production company in Los Angeles, that used good equipment. All of it was owned—purchased with a bank loan. The monthly bills were staggering and the company found that it needed to produce programs for virtually anybody who walked in the door in order to keep its loan payments current. One week we might be working on an excellent documentary project for a major Christian leader, and the next, we were out shooting tennis lessons at the local high school. The atmosphere of the company was always frantic, as the owners were constantly on the lookout for new business to pay the bills.

Across town was another producer who created similar types of programming, but he rented his equipment. During a shoot the equipment cost him a little more, but after a production, he turned it in, and was able to relax, and mentally and creatively prepare for the next project. He always had access the latest state-of-the-art tools, since each time he rented equipment he was able to choose exactly what types of gear he needed, and could choose the latest models. Furthermore, he had the great luxury of only doing work for the quality clients that were within the scope of what he wanted to do in life, which was produce and direct quality television and film projects for Christian clients.

Now admittedly, a church or ministry situation is somewhat different. Unless you are planning to produce programs only periodically, you will probably find it more cost effective over the long haul to purchase, since you will be using your equipment regularly, week in and week out.

I do suggest, however, that you give serious consideration to buying as little equipment as possible—at least until you are absolutely sure of the stability and the future of your program. Earlier we discussed outsourcing. This could be exactly the type of situation for which outsourcing would be perfect. This allows you to keep your expenses down and also to take advantage of the latest changes in technology.

Buying Equipment on a Lease/Purchase Option

This approach works the same way lease/purchase agreements work in other fields: in most cases, your lease payments apply to the eventual purchase of the equipment. The advantage of this approach is that should you desire to change equipment, after discovering that you haven't made the right selection after all, you can still do so. And if you made the right choice, at least your lease payments are applying toward the purchase.

But remember, in this environment where technological changes happen every day, it isn't unusual to lease your equipment, period. There's no more drag on a ministry's finances that a television studio full of out-of-date, purchased equipment. But keep in mind, every situation is different. So keep all of your options open and heed the advice of equipment experts, media consultants, and financial associates before you make a large financial commitment.

Where Do You Find Equipment?

The television equipment industry is growing as never before, and with the advent of religious and corporate broadcasting, the competition among vendors has increased. This has brought the equipment costs down and quality up.

Television equipment and rental companies exist in almost every major city in America, and where they don't exist, the proper equipment for your purposes can usually be brought in on overnight notice. Don't be afraid to shop around, and don't be afraid to get bids from a number of sources. The important thing is not to be impressed with flash, free giveaways, fancy gadgetry, or fast talk. Look for a dealer who is not only prepared to make you a good financial deal, but who is concerned about your program and wants to make certain that you get exactly the right equipment in order to do the job successfully.

Bear in mind that the video equipment salesman may be an expert on the *technical* features of the equipment he sells, but he is probably not a *program producer*. I strongly suggest that you include your creative team in the decisions about equipment.

A car salesman at least drives a car everyday and not only knows how it's built, but how it drives. However, a video salesman usually knows how the equipment is built, but rarely has used it himself in the production of an actual program. I am not criticizing equipment salesmen. Most of the dealers I've encountered are highly reputable and will offer valuable advice on your rental or purchase. I do, however, think that the people who will use your equipment every day will give you another valuable perspective as well.

One of the best places to window shop for equipment is the annual National Association of Broadcasters Convention.

The NAB Convention is held in a major city (usually Las Vegas) every spring, and it truly is the biggest event for television and radio equipment dealers in the world. In one place you can see the major equipment manufacturers and dealers not only display their equipment, but operate it for you as well. Many of the camera manufacturers, for example, actually build a studio and bring in professional models to shoot so you can see how each camera operates. The companies that build and sell lights, videotape, recording equipment, post equipment, and all of the vast supporting services and equipment are at the NAB. I highly recommend a visit before you begin to seriously discuss equipment with vendors in your area. In fact, if you are already talking to equipment companies, they may very well provide passes for you to the NAB just to demonstrate their products!

For more information about this conference, contact:

The National Association of Broadcasters on the web at www.nab.org.

Or contact your equipment dealer, local television station, or production company.

Above all, I suggest that you avail yourself of a hands-on demonstration for any equipment you are seriously considering. (Rarely do you buy a car without a test drive.)

In fact, most dealers will bring a prospective piece of equipment into your facility, hook it up, and let you use it for a time to see how it works within your program.

But above all, remember that a dealer can talk about signal-to-noise ratio, lines of resolution, harmonic distortion, modulation, or clip levels, but what it all comes down to is this: will this piece of equipment work well for you—for your purposes, in your situation, within your budget, and with your people, to accomplish your goals?

I also suggest that when you go in for a hands-on demonstration and as you are about to enter final consideration of *any* piece of equipment, take someone with you whom you trust to give you a straight opinion about the effectiveness and price of the equipment, even if you have to pay them to go along.

Before we leave this discussion about purchasing equipment, I want to answer a final question that I receive on a regular basis: "What about buying used equipment?"

Television equipment is a highly fluctuating field because the technology changes so rapidly. What is the best today, may be nearly worthless tomorrow. Because of that fact, buying used equipment can be a very tricky business.

I'm all for buying used equipment as long as certain considerations are strictly adhered to:

     —Get an accurate appraisal of the performance and value from a third party.

     —Find out if the continued maintenance of the equipment will be worth the savings.

     —Find out if the original manufacturer is still making parts and servicing the equipment.

     Cameras are a good example. There are some terrific buys out there for used cameras. The only problem is that many of those *great buys* are cameras that need constant maintenance. If that's not a problem for you, then look into it, but if you're like most people, it's just not worth the additional effort.

     Compared with today's cameras, which are almost zero maintenance and tough as nails, it may be more than worth it to spend a little more and get a new camera.

State-of-the-Art

     The term *state-of-the-art* is thrown around television as much as in any other technical field and I feel sure you'll hear it often as you begin to scout out equipment. Ideally, this term means that the piece of equipment *is the latest and most technologically superior item on the market.* In reality, it is more often a matter of perception.

     Don't believe that everything you see is state-of-the-art. Chances are true state-of-the-art equipment is actually much more advanced, and is still in someone's research and development department down the street.

One of the fastest changing areas today is post-production equipment. In the past fifteen years, just about everything in the post-production arena has changed dramatically. The quality, availability, and price are vastly more favorable. Yet even as you buy, bear in mind that state-of-the-art today might be out-of-date tomorrow.

Make a choice you can live with, because state-of-the-art is a risk. You will only have *state-of-the-art* equipment for awhile. You will have *workhorse* equipment for a lot longer. Your challenge is to make sure the new model you buy today will last, and that it is part of an integrated system or in a sequence of upgrades. (You'll find that companies don't reinvent the entire wheel each year, but they come up with new innovations every quarter, six months, or year. Look for something that has the potential of being upgraded for an extended life.)

The three factors you should consider most strongly are:

1) **Service:** Can I get the equipment serviced easily? How inexpensively? Can I get spare parts?

2) **Price:** "Most expensive" isn't always best. "Least expensive" isn't always cheapest—by the time you've repaired it a dozen times. Weigh track records of similar equipment against the price. Virtually everything is negotiable, especially if you are putting together a package of several types of equipment or are outfitting a small studio.

3) **Flexibility:** Will the piece of equipment be compatible with other pieces of equipment? Can it move from one location to another or must it be permanently mounted? Are there great numbers of people out there who know how to operate it? Is it a relatively common piece of equipment in comparable facilities?

Packages vs. Components

Consider the last time you went shopping for a home entertainment system. You probably noticed quickly that one name brand offered just about everything that went together to make a system: DVD player, CD player, cassette player, receiver, amplifier, speakers, surround sound, everything in one neat little package.

When you go to a top-of-the-line, high-end stereo shop, however, things are a little different. You see many more *component* pieces and fewer *package* set-ups. One company specializes in the very best CD players, another has the best speakers, another has the best turntables, and so forth.

Television equipment is very much like the second example. Very few companies (if any) make everything you need, and very few quality studios are outfitted from one source. One company may specialize in cameras, another in audio gear, another in lights, another in non-linear editing equipment, and another in switchers.

In broadcast television, I am very skeptical of most package deals. The best studios I have seen are those where each component was the best in its field. I also should interject that in many cases *best* is a subjective term. Technology is at such a level today that many companies have outstanding equipment. When I use *best* in regard to equipment, I very often mean best for the particular application. In other words, one camera is best in a studio, one is best on location, one is best for specialty applications, etc.

I'll never forget being invited on a tour of a local church's television facility in the upper Midwest. This pastor was especially proud because everything in his studio had come from a single company. The company was so happy that they did a feature story on the church's newly installed facility in their company magazine. The pastor was excited as he showed me the magazine article on his facility.

But the truth was, although that company did make certain excellent pieces of television equipment, others were very substandard and inadequate. He had been convinced by the salesman without ever consulting any actual working engineers, and consequently, had spent hundreds of thousands of dollars—much of it wasted on poor equipment.

Choosing equipment that fits together and finding the best elements for your purposes may take a little more effort and time on your part, but it will be well worth it.

Most dealers represent many lines of equipment anyway, so if you work through a reputable dealer or consultant, this is not a problem.

The Chief or Consulting Engineer

One of the most important people to include in your discussions about equipment *before you buy* is the engineer for your program or studio. Ultimately, this person will be an important resource in hiring all technical personnel, and the key to maintaining and operating all equipment in your television facility. That's a major role that should not be taken lightly.

137

In many facilities, this is a full-time position, but in others, it's a freelance consulting or maintenance engineer brought in occasionally when problems arise.

As in any production situation, the responsibilities of the engineer-in-charge may vary. In some situations, he is merely a manager and does not directly operate or maintain the equipment. In other cases, he is a video operator, a videotape editor, or fills some other position on the engineering or production staff.

In either event, he should be an experienced engineer with an extensive background in electronics, and experience and in-depth knowledge of television specifically. I can't say enough about the importance of good engineering and maintenance to get the most out of your equipment, keep your program looking and sounding its best, and maintain a proper and correct air signal. It's not only vital, but it's a legal requirement to adhere to FCC standards, and it takes the acquisition of proper equipment and monitoring devices to check the signal accurately.

In a television or radio broadcast station, the chief engineer is normally required to have an upper-level Federal Communications Commission (FCC) license. But in most studios or production situations, that isn't necessary.

As I stated before, your engineer doesn't have to be a full-time employee. This depends on the size of your facility, the amount of equipment to be maintained, and your overall level of production. In fact, many ministries use another facility's full-time engineer to occasionally moonlight at night.

Remember the National Association of Broadcasters Conference we discussed earlier? I strongly suggest you take a television engineer to the NAB conference with you. You'll learn a great deal from listening to him ask questions, watching him try out the equipment, and explaining all the various equipment details and options.

Your director gets your program ready to broadcast.

Your engineer makes certain that your program can be broadcast, and in the case of *live* broadcasts, he keeps you on the air.

Engineers are often the unsung heroes of television.

Chapter Six

Reaching an Audience

"Go ye into all the world, and preach the gospel to every creature."

Mark 16:15

"When we asked viewers how much money it would take to get them to stop watching TV, more than a quarter said either a million dollars or that they would not stop watching TV for any amount of money."

Channels Magazine

Television in some form or another is here to stay. So why do programs come and go so quickly?

Tastes change and audiences are fickle. Never lose sight of those overriding facts.

You may be under the assumption that the world is just waiting for your program, but chances are it isn't. You are going to have to work hard to get your program on the air, and even harder to get viewers to tune in. You might have—on videotape—the greatest program ever produced. But until that program is seen by enough people, you haven't succeeded.

So how do you go about finding your audience?

The first move is to investigate exactly where you want to broadcast your programs. There are many different outlets these days, just as there are different ways to sell books, cars, and just about everything else. You primarily need to ask: *Where is my audience?*

What About Working With Individual Television Stations?

This is the oldest way of "broadcasting" a television program. On a nationwide scale, ministers such as Rex Humbard, Billy Graham, and Oral Roberts pioneered this method in the 1950's, and even today, this is usually the place where the greatest audiences lie waiting.

As of this writing, cable television, for all its phenomenal growth in the last few years, still doesn't quite reach the audience that broadcast television networks reach. But cable's influence is continuing to grow at remarkable rates, and it's only a matter of time.

There are basically three ways of getting a program aired on traditional broadcast stations:

1) Send the program via signal, satellite or otherwise, to network affiliates around the country. They, in turn, broadcast the signal to their viewership area. (This is the way the secular networks NBC, CBS, ABC and FOX, as well as Christian networks like Daystar, INSP, TLN, and TBN do it.)

2) Work with station groups or ad-hoc networks. These are stations that have come together either in a formal business relationship or a handshake deal to broadcast common programs throughout their combined reach.

3) The other way is to approach each television station separately, work out a contract regarding the time slot for the program, and the price for that slot, and then send a separate videotape of your program each week to that station.

Sound complicated? It is.

With the exception of programs that air exclusively on Christian networks, most of the Christian programs you see regularly on Sunday mornings use this third method. At one time, some were sending as many as 100-200 separate videotapes to stations across the nation each week, but today program distribution is usually done via satellite. In these cases, duplicating, shipping, and satellite costs play a major role in their program budgets. But arrangements still have to be made with each individual station to record the program off the satellite feed at the correct time each week.

A problem quickly arises in keeping track of that many individual stations, including billing, advertising and promotion, contract status, time charges and the general paperwork regarding these issues. In order to farm out some of this work, most major ministries use media or time buyers—agencies or individuals who specialize in representing your organization to the individual stations and networks across the nation.

These representatives are people who know the markets. They work with stations every day and keep track of what time slots are opening and closing, how much to pay for each, and how to negotiate successfully with station managers.

For instance, a time buy during the prime-time evening period is considerably more expensive to purchase than a slot earlier in the day or later at night. The same holds true for special periods such as Sunday afternoon sporting events, Saturday mornings, and so forth. Each day is broken up into sections called *day parts*, based on how many viewers are watching at that particular time. Basically, your *media* buyer could be more accurately called an *audience* buyer.

The larger the audience, the more expensive the time.

The media buyer makes his money from a 15% commission paid out from the television or cable station. Can you make the media buy yourself and save the 15%? You can make the media buy yourself, but you probably won't save the 15%. In fact, you'll probably pay more. The stations look to media buyers to bring a large number of clients to them, and therefore a 15% commission is viewed as an incentive for business. On the other hand, the station probably won't extend you the same commission, since you don't bring them much business. Besides, a media buyer does this for a living, and is constantly looking for better timeslots, channels, and placement. Believe me, that 15% commission is earned, and the advice and counsel you get from an established media buyer is more than worth the money.

One of the biggest mistakes I see in Christian media is managers of church or ministry media departments trying to "save" the ministry money by firing the media buyer and trying to do it in-house. In almost every case, the church or ministry ends up actually paying more for the same time, losing valuable timeslots to competitors, and dropping viewers because of ineptly handled time purchases. The bottom line?

Let a professional do it.

Individual broadcast stations remain the most established outlets for religious programming, although cable networks are not far behind. In most cases, depending on the time slot you want, broadcast stations are going to be the most expensive option.

One of the biggest surprises you may have as you enter the world of television production is the price of TV time. Competition is fierce in many markets, and often this competition is hottest among Christian ministries. Losing a time slot to a higher bidder can mean hundreds of thousands and even millions of dollars in lost revenue over the years. But staying up with the rising prices can also create a real money challenge for your ministry.

What If You Are Just Starting Out?

You are probably going to begin with a local station or cable channel, and you generally don't need a time-buying representative. I often suggest that you place the time yourself. That's especially true if you know a local businessman who has some experience in advertising or buying commercial time for his own business. You'd be surprised at the members in your church or on your board who are local car dealers or retail store owners who have experience or contacts dealing with the local television stations.

In most cases, professional media buyers come into play when you're ready to move out of your local market and explore multi-station or network options.

Low Power Stations

Relatively recently in the span of broadcasting, the federal government has opened up an entirely new type of broadcast station called *"low power."* In simple terms, a low-power station is exactly what it says: it broadcasts like a normal station, but with power to reach only a small coverage area.

Because it is cheaper to own and operate a low-power station, the federal government has encouraged women, minorities, and those in rural areas to get involved in this new type of broadcasting. It is now possible, for example, for a small town in the Texas panhandle to have its own television station, and to provide its own local news, sports, weather, and locally-produced programs.

It's an exciting prospect, because low-power stations will reach a new audience with a more personal touch than ever before. The facilities and equipment are relatively easy to operate and maintain. Christian broadcasters—and particularly those with smaller ministries and churches who want to reach a specific region—should seriously consider these outlets.

Time cost is a fraction of that for larger stations, and in rural areas, there is remarkable loyalty to these stations from local viewers.

A few attempts have been made to link up low-power stations across the nation into some kind of network, but few organizations to date have had much success. Some Christian broadcasting networks have moved in that direction, but for most, it's been rather difficult. I suspect that the very nature and diversity of the audiences and locations may keep this from happening. At the same time, I see support for these stations growing, and a new Christian ministry can do well on these stations with the right buys in the right slots.

Although in many cases it may be important to consider buying time on low-power stations, should you be a *minority* church or ministry, I would suggest you especially inquire about *purchasing* one or more of these stations. At the time of this writing, the government is encouraging purchases—especially by minority owners. Depending on a number of variables, it may be a great opportunity for a minority Christian broadcaster. *(Contact the Federal Communications Commission in Washington, D.C. for more information).*

Cable Television

After broadcast stations, including both full- and low-power, your next alternative is *cable.*

Cable television's expansion during the last decade has been explosive. 500 channel systems are now a reality, although we're already seeing some major corporate shifts because of financial changes within the industry. In addition, we're now seeing the phone companies get into the act, and major computer companies and Internet providers are already talking about program distribution through a combination of broadband Internet/cable services.

Because of these developments, I strongly believe that we have moved beyond the network days into an era where viewers will have a greater choice of programs for any one time period on any given day. This is not to say, however, that the networks are doomed. Even they recognize these new directions, as evidenced by their major investments in cable channels and networks.

Simply put, what is happening in cable television today is very similar to what happened to the magazine publishing industry 25 years ago. Look at any well-appointed newsstand today, and you will find an unbelievable number of titles. But even beyond the newsstand, you'll find hundreds, even thousands, of titles that reach highly specialized audiences. As each magazine gets more and more specialized, it in turn reaches a smaller and smaller segment of the audience. But because our society is highly segmented, that does not mean that these smaller, more specialized magazines are in financial difficulty. To the contrary. Many of them are among the most solid financial ventures.

Now look at your particular cable television guidebook. It is not uncommon to find upwards of 100 channels. In fact, I recently attended a seminar to discuss the programming implications of the larger 500-channel systems. One channel for rock-and-roll music, another for country music, a couple of religious channels, a sports channel or two, a few movie channels, a news channel, a financial channel, an arts channel, a weather channel, and much more. The more segments, the smaller the audience for each.

Years ago, a Christian program could pretty much draw on most of the Christians in the community, but not anymore. Today, young people want their own programs, gospel music fans want theirs, Bible

147

students want teaching programs, families want programs they can enjoy together, the list goes on and on.

What does this mean to you? It means that cable distribution may be your best bet. Why?

Your costs will probably be lower, since it's less-expensive to purchase time. And your audience will probably be smaller, but if you know the market, they may be a more committed audience for your type of program. So your greatest challenge will be to find a segment of the market and hit it "on target."

But how do you go about it?

The Importance of Television Demographics

Demographics is the statistical study of human populations, especially with reference to their size, density, distribution, and vital statistics. In television, demographics refers to where your audience is, who they are, and when they are watching.

Television research companies such as Nielsen and formerly Arbitron have, over the years, made very successful businesses out of providing producers with exactly this type of information. Wall Street has made millions from the study of demographics. Hollywood rises and falls by it. And you can greatly benefit by knowing a profile of your viewers—gender, age, income levels, locations, and so forth.

In some cases, your TV audiences may mirror almost exactly your direct-mail audience, congregation, or partnership as a whole. In other cases, you may be surprised to find that a number of people are watching you but aren't corresponding with you. (That's a good place to seek answers to a "why not" question!)

The value of ratings services is that they can tell you how many people are watching in particular areas of the country. As you grow, this will become vital information. There's no point in buying an expensive time slot in Detroit, for example, if you have few viewers there. Spend your money in Dallas, perhaps, where you have more viewers!

However, I would add a word of caution before you jump on the audience ratings bandwagon. There is a great deal of controversy over the current techniques used in audience ratings. While some people feel they are extremely accurate, others feel that the ratings services are highly inaccurate to the point of being ridiculous. In Hollywood, you'll generally find the networks crusading on the side of the ratings companies and the producers strongly against them. The networks need something to help them create a scale for selling airtime, but the program producers feel that the current techniques aren't good enough for a real understanding of viewing habits.

One thing is for certain, unless your audience numbers at least into the hundreds of thousands of viewers, the numbers of any ratings service will probably not accurately reflect your real audience.

Therefore, you won't need these services for awhile, especially if you are just starting out. For a more in-depth discussion of demographics and audience ratings, I would encourage you to consult a media buyer.

What About Free or Inexpensive Airtime?

In the first few years of cable television, many people rushed to buy cable channels even though there wasn't yet enough programming to go around. They often offered free time just to fill up their schedules.

Today, this situation is not nearly as prevalent, although in some parts of the country where cable is still evolving and still being established, you might still find a channel offering greatly reduced time fees or even free time. Bear in mind, however, that there are no "free lunches." Don't leap at an offering of free airtime as an irresistible notion. You may find yourself spending lots of money on the production of shows that no one is watching. In that case, you have wasted your money, even though the time was "free."

After all, with the exception of fulfilling public service requirements, if the time slot was so terrific, why would the station be giving it away?

Pilot Programs

A pilot is a test program, and as a producer, I heartily recommend that you consider them. A pilot gives you an opportunity to see if your ideas will work. Watch TV in the summer and you'll see lots of pilots that were prepared for the fall series. Some are two-hour pilots under the guise of movies, but they're really a test-run for a new series. It also allows you the opportunity to work out the "bugs" with a new crew and equipment.

Think of a pilot as part of your *research and development* effort. Most companies have an R&D department in order to experiment with new products and test them before rolling them out to the masses. It's a good idea for ministries to adopt.

If you've ever been involved in the making of a television program, you know that there's nothing like seeing a finished product. The script doesn't tell you, the set design doesn't tell you, even the quality of performers won't tell you, and the director can't tell you, what a finished product will show you.

You may be wise to do a pilot in order to have something to take with you under your arm as you go from station to station to attempt to buy time for a new program. (In fact, you will probably need just such a program if you have never been on television before. Remember the director's demo tape? Your pilot will become your program's demo tape.)

Attempt to make your pilot as much like the program you envision as possible. There are no excuses that will work when it comes time for a station manager to view your prospective show. They will assume this is the first of many shows and that all of the others are at least similar to the one they are watching.

The station manager won't care that your lighting equipment hadn't arrived yet, or the new microphones didn't work, or that you had a bad day in the pulpit. Whatever you do, don't show anyone a pilot that isn't the best example of producing a program you're capable of. For instance, I know of stations and networks that view new programs once or twice a year—and once they've seen it, they will not watch a program

151

again, even a re-edited or updated version. Therefore, it has to be right the first time.

Give the pilot your best shot, so it isn't your *only* shot!

Direct Broadcast Satellites (DBS)

At one time it was believed that DBS was the future of broadcasting. But with the advent of 500-channel cable, pay-per-view, and broadband, it may not play the role many originally thought. For awhile, it looked like DBS was dead, but companies like Direct-TV, the DISH Network, and Sky Angel revived the concept and now it's off and running once again.

There's a lot of experimentation and talk going on today about other potential direct programming services, and there are those in Christian circles who are already producing programming and transmitting it directly to satellites for individual churches and organizations to pull down. (In these situations, the audience must purchase a satellite receiving dish that enables them to receive a particular event produced by a central organization.)

Using this concept, a rural church or an organization that cannot otherwise afford highly trained speakers or singers of national prominence, can receive a "live" service from another location, and participate in it as the others lead, even adding whatever else they want to the program to create their own "custom" service. I personally believe that this is a very exciting possibility, but the event has to be created with that technology in mind. Otherwise, it's no different than what you'll find on Christian television, and there's no reason for church members to leave home.

Direct Satellite Broadcasting will continue to use smaller and smaller dishes (more like the size of an umbrella or even a serving platter) that will enable individual homes to subscribe to the programs of their choice. In many ways, it will be a wireless version of current pay-per-view or multi-channel cable.

The greatest drawback for direct services is the lack of interactivity. With computer and phone companies setting up interactive programming possibilities, old fashioned "wired" service is currently the only way that signals can effectively go back and forth and make that happen.

Advertising

Advertising is important. Don't let anybody convince you otherwise, especially if you're just starting out. "Word of mouth" isn't going to get you an audience big enough, or fast enough to make your program a success.

As I write this manuscript, the networks are announcing that commercials during this year's Super Bowl will sell for $1.2 million per 30 seconds. That's a testament to the power of advertising!

Good advertising is a craft. Don't think that because your nephew writes well, he can handle the advertising for your ministry. Mistakes can be expensive. I suggest that you find a good advertising agency, or at least a veteran freelancer who has a track record. A traditional agency will charge a negotiable 15 percent commission on the services they provide, but this is still cheaper than hiring a newcomer and having to train them—especially if that person makes mistakes at your expense.

Look for an agency the same way you look for a television producer or a media consultant. Ask for a demo reel of their television work. In the case of print advertising, ask for a portfolio. These will contain samples of the quality of their work, and give you an idea of the personality of the agency and of their products.

I wouldn't limit your search to just Christian advertising agencies, but the fact is, there are many excellent Christian agencies. The directory of the *National Religious Broadcasters*, which is listed in the appendix of this book, will be a good reference for that purpose.

Generally, you will work with an agency this way:

1) You will meet with them initially to exchange ideas and information. At this time, they may want to make a presentation to convince you that they're the best agency for the job. Up to this point the relationship has cost you nothing.

2) The agency will then generally make a preliminary presentation to you about their original ideas. They may charge you for the time or expense it takes to do this. You can ask for a rough or a complete look. The price will vary accordingly. Bear in mind that the agency is taking a risk in showing you their ideas, and that's why they are likely to ask for payment for their time.

3) Should you decide to enter into a relationship with the agency, you will hire them on a contract basis or a retainer basis. "Contract" is generally per production (such as a television special or a series of ads that comprise a campaign). A "retainer" is a monthly fee paid (usually with a cost-plus feature) to have them do ongoing work for you.

Remember that you hold the final say. Don't be snowed by a flashy look if that isn't what you want to convey to your audience. Make sure the agency understands your ministry's motivations and goals and reflects that vision in their work.

Agencies in turn hire artists, writers, buyers, account specialists, and others who will take your advertising into the marketplace and put them in the right places to reach your target audience. Many agencies have time-buying departments as well. In these cases, you may be killing two birds with one stone—*they can do your advertising and promotion as well as handle your program's airtime.*

As in the case of freelance producers, you will also find *freelance* artists and writers available to help if you decide not to follow the traditional agency route. Either way, make sure you find someone who can convey in advertising the excitement, quality, and vision you are trying to portray in your program.

Freelancers are considerably less expensive and may be the best approach as you begin your television ministry. Many outstanding writers and artists are working on their own with the help of computers, fax machines, cellular phones, and so forth. *Why pay for the overhead of a big agency?* In fact, recently in Los Angeles, one of the largest and most successful advertising agencies bought their creative staff notebook computers and cell phones, then sent them home. They found the quality of work was better in the relaxed atmosphere of a home office, and the reduced office space significantly lowered expenses, which could be passed on directly to the client.

Perhaps Ford, GM, Levi's, Shell, Delta and others can afford it, but you probably need to think in more innovative terms to keep your costs down.

The decision is ultimately whether you need to start on a smaller budget and can find the quality freelancers to handle the job, or use a traditional agency where all the services are under one roof.

Either way, make sure that your vision permeates your entire outreach, including the work that agencies do for you.

As in all other areas of a television ministry, you need to be involved in determining where you want your programs broadcast and how you want them advertised. You need to take a special role in preparing the pilot program. Don't stand by and expect others to read your mind, or they may read something into your ministry that you haven't intended! Work with these people to help them understand what it is that you want to accomplish, and what the parameters are for getting the job done.

Full Service Advertising Agencies

In the media world, there are a variety of companies and combinations of services. Some advertising agencies are called "full service agencies" and combine advertising, marketing, production, graphic design, and media buying all under one roof. Other companies take a more specialized approach and only do one thing.

Which is better? Every case is different. Some companies specialize because they want to achieve extraordinarily high levels of expertise in a single area. In other cases, full service agencies can give your church or ministry a theme throughout all the advertising, marketing, production, or media buying they create. Your media consultant can guide you, but only make a decision after you feel confident about their ability to translate your vision into the marketplace.

Chapter Seven

Financing Your Television Outreach

"For the worker deserves his wages."

Luke 10:7

"The two most beautiful words in the English language are: check enclosed."

Novelist Dorothy Parker

Now for some real controversy: *finances.* The art and strategy of raising money to pay for the programs you produce and broadcast.

Let's look at the numbers. A typical broadcast camera can cost between $15,000 and $150,000, an amazingly wide range, depending on the quality, resolution, and most important, the lens. That's for one camera. Most directors today use at least three, and some as many as eight cameras or more.

That's just for cameras.

Add videotape recorders, audio equipment, lighting equipment, crew labor, post-production equipment—the list is a long one.

And then there's broadcast airtime. For a nationally broadcast *daily* television program, you can easily spend $10,000, $20,000, $30,000, or more per day just for airtime. That doesn't include advertising and promotion.

Are you still with me?

The point is, *television costs money.* Lots and lots of it.

And if you've ever wondered why so many ministers on television preach about giving in so many programs, make a budget, hope you figured everything in, add a little to be safe, and you'll start to understand.

Actually, the much-criticized image of a TV minister begging for money is not actually rooted in reality, especially today. While some television preachers and ministries do spend a great deal of time raising money, the vast majority of ministries *(including some that are strongly criticized on this point by the secular media)* actually make fundraising a tiny part of each program—often having less than five percent of the program being devoted to "taking the offering."

Nevertheless, there is no question that some ministries terribly abuse fundraising both over the air and through their direct mail. Those ministries have left a terrible stigma on Christian broadcasting that may never completely disappear. But in spite of the cases of abuse, studies indicate that overall, fundraising by religious broadcasters takes up far fewer minutes per hour than the commercial spots aired on the secular networks.

Still, it takes money to be on television, and somehow, you'll need to raise it.

I want to make an important editorial point before we get into the discussion. *I am not a professional fundraiser. I am a television producer and media consultant.* But because of the expensive nature of producing Christian programs today an effective producer understands the need to work closely with professionals who understand the art of fundraising.

Through those relationships over the years, I have seen the important need for professional fundraising techniques within a ministry setting. Raising money for television is something that can't be left to chance.

The following discussion is not meant to be a textbook on fundraising. Through the years, fundraising techniques have changed, and the art of raising money through ministries is constantly being re-thought and re-worked. In fact, I've discovered that different ministry supporters have different personalities, and giving patterns vary a great deal from ministry to ministry. I am constantly amazed at how important it is to change techniques as I work with different churches and ministries.

Some ministries and successful churches do no television fundraising at all. I know of a very successful television pastor whom I respect very much who uses television as a mission field. His church congregation has taken it upon itself to finance the television outreach, and he never has to ask for money on the air. (Never forget though, he still has to raise the money through his church members, so the indirect need for fundraising is still there.)

Nevertheless, the following discussion is meant to help you start thinking about the issues involved in raising money for your television ministry, whether you do it on television, through direct mail, through product sales, through your congregation, or through any other arena. Since this is a basic text, the overall idea I want to convey is that financing your television ministry is serious business, and you have to approach fundraising as a thoughtful task.

What About Advertising?

Historically, ministries have been highly reluctant to seek outside advertising and use commercial spots within their programs. Today, some are trying valiantly to reverse that trend, but that model has been in place so long, it will be difficult to do.

But we must continue to try.

In virtually all sponsorship situations today, the sponsoring companies have very little input into the content of the program being produced. If a pharmaceutical firm wanted to run an aspirin commercial during a Christian television program, I'm not at all convinced that it would hurt the program in any way. As long as the company or product does not interfere with a minister's message, or the values of the program, sponsorship can be a valid means for paying all or part of the costs of producing and broadcasting a program.

This tendency to avoid sponsorship is a matter of tradition, based on the fact that in the early days of television, sponsors had much more to do with the actual production of programs. During the "Golden Age of Television" in the 1940's and 1950's, sponsors had direct control over the script, the producer, casting, and many other aspects of program production. When the early Christian broadcasters came on the scene in the mid-1950's, they rightly had no desire to have a sponsoring company take any control over their message or the content of the programs. To preserve the integrity of their message, they decided to just buy the time slot directly and pay for it themselves, which led to the birth of what we call today "paid time" programming.

161

It was an important step during those early days, but today that trend for sponsor control has changed. Most advertisers just want to sponsor programs that deliver a significant viewing audience, and have little or no interest in the actual content of the program. The problem is, most Christian broadcasters have not changed with it. And today, Madison Avenue doesn't think of Christian broadcasting in terms of a large enough audience to justify sponsorship. In spite of the enormous growth of Christian networks and stations over the last two decades, pitching our programming to advertisers is still a tough sell.

During the tragic years when a number of major television ministries collapsed due to various moral, ethical, and legal problems, some of their books were opened to the public. When advertising agencies saw the enormous amount of money some of those ministries were making through their television programs and the large audience numbers involved, the agencies were intrigued, and for a short time considered advertising on Christian programming. However, the negative baggage those ministries represented to the American public at that time was enough reason for agencies to be cautious, so they never actually pursued the idea.

Nevertheless, many producers are still trying, and because of that, selling advertising time is something to consider—especially at the local level. As you begin your television ministry, there's no question that you should approach local businesses—especially those who may be members of your congregation or partners in your ministry—to sponsor your broadcast with commercial spots.

I know churches with members who own large furniture stores, bookstores, insurance companies, and other businesses, and in some cases, they advertise locally on the church program. Running a commercial spot or two during a broadcast is so normal for TV viewers that few will think anything about it, and the revenue generated from the advertiser takes much of the pressure off raising money on the air.

On the other hand, not everyone feels as strongly about advertising in Christian programs. Today, there are a number of pastors, evangelists, and church leaders who believe just as strongly that the public needs to give in order to open up their lives to the power of God and to have a part in extending the gospel to an unsaved world. Others feel that advertising would damage the integrity of preaching the gospel on television.

However, remember that Christian radio has almost always been advertiser based, and the successful number of ministries on radio indicates that those advertisers haven't done any damage to the integrity of the gospel in that medium.

That choice gets into a personal spiritual area, and you will ultimately have to decide for yourself. But whatever way you choose, you will need financing to operate a successful television or radio ministry.

In discussing fundraising, the main points for you to consider are these:

1) You are going to have to think seriously about fundraising right now. It's not something you can "hope works out." The financial needs will be too great.

2) Ultimately, you are going to have to become informed, skilled, and successful in the particular funding techniques that will work for your ministry (your audience, your goals, your program). You'll have to discover what works well for you, and you'll have to do it early on in your development.

3) Whatever techniques you use, will have to have integrity, and not embarrass the faith you represent, your ministry or Christian broadcasting in general.

Fundraising

Let's begin by separating "asking for an offering" from "fundraising." For our purposes, *asking for an offering* is an identical appeal that goes out to everyone (just as in a church setting). In other words, the congregation is asked to give to meet a particular ongoing need and then the offering plate is passed down the row.

Fundraising, on the other hand, involves a definite set of principles and techniques that, when used correctly, can be far more effective.

There are some basic concepts related to fundraising that I invite you to think about as you consider the future of your own ministry:

Principle #1

Don't be afraid to ask

Don't assume that your viewers will know you need money. Don't assume that they know the costs of airtime and production. After all, they don't pay for television, at least not in a way they recognize. Few realize that several cents on the cost of every product they purchase in the grocery store actually goes toward paying for advertising and the commercials they watch on TV. They have no idea that they should pay for the privilege of watching Christian television, and therefore there is nothing wrong with educating them on that fact. The question is not really about asking, but about asking with integrity, graciousness, and purpose.

Principle #2

Recognize that each member of your audience is at a different giving level

Some can give $500 or more. For some, $5 is a strain. You need to recognize that everyone has a different level for giving and present each person with an opportunity to give in a meaningful way at their particular level. By meaningful, I mean the person must find a sense of fulfillment, purpose, and accomplishment in his or her gift, no matter how small.

I recently watched a minister present a project on television and the only amount of money he asked for was $100. It was linked to a specific project, and he gave the audience no other options.

Now very few people in a mass viewing audience *can or will* give $100, unless they are already your committed supporters.

What happened to this minister?

Very few people responded.

Those who *could have* given $10, $20, $30, $40, didn't because the minister had specifically named a figure out of their reach or desire. And those who could have given $1,000 or even $10,000 still only gave $100 because that's what the minister asked for.

He severely limited his potential by focusing solely on one financial level. He made a serious mistake. I have to admit, he did have one aspect of fundraising correct: *you need to ask and to ask specifically.*

But he missed the mark by not giving options.

Having said that, there will be times when you need to ask for specific amounts for specific reasons. A media consultant or professional fundraiser can educate you on those options, but at this stage, it's critical to know that different people are capable of giving different amounts, and your fundraising program should be able to accommodate those variations.

Principle #3

Give people the opportunity to support your project

The best projects have multiple facets, each of which can be tied to a dollar amount. For example, let's suppose that you are sponsoring the building of your television studio. Few people can afford to give the entire amount. Therefore, the best approach may be to breakdown the elements of the studio into affordable levels of giving.

For instance, a small group of viewers could give to purchase a videotape machine, a single person could give for a box of videotape, or others could give to purchase lighting equipment. Individually, it doesn't add up to much, but corporately, you can build a television studio.

The key is to break down your projects into affordable pieces at varying levels. And each piece must be important to the whole! No one wants to give for something that seems unimportant.

That's a crucial point. *Every aspect of your presentation must be perceived as useful and meaningful.*

"But why do I need a project at all?"

Because the average person is not motivated toward giving for general operating expenses. I wish it weren't true, but it is. People respond to building or to those projects that demonstrate you are doing something to meet a specific need. They give to activities, missions of mercy, building programs, and similar endeavors.

People do not like giving to erase debt.

People do not like giving for your payroll.

People do not like giving for maintenance and upkeep projects.

Now they sometimes do, and they have, and they will, but they generally won't make it a habit. And what you need more than anything in the world are people who will make it a habit to give to your ministry.

Another Approach

There is an alternate approach that has been used quite heavily during the last few decades—*giving to receive*, based on the principles of what's called "seed faith." Oral Roberts created this teaching in the 1950's and 1960's and it's exploded throughout media ministries ever since. In other words, the viewer doesn't give to a particular project or to accomplish a task for the Kingdom of God, they give in order to receive something in return from God. This is usually tied into a ministry whose central focus is planting seeds, or teaching people the value of giving.

This book isn't a theological debate on the merits of giving, or different approaches to fundraising, but I do want to point out that there are a number of ministries that use this approach—some with success, and some without.

Depending on your particular ministry, you may or may not want to explore that alternative. Although I do believe in the Biblical principles of giving, I also know that this has been an area that has experienced abuse, criticism, and controversy in the past.

The fact is, the Bible does spend considerable time teaching on money, and yet many pastors seem to ignore those sections of the scripture. Considering the fact that money is the basis of most transactions in our society, and surveys indicate that Christians typically have as many money problems as those in secular society, I do think pastors and teachers should engage this issue on a deeper basis. Whether or not you believe in the concept of seed faith, prosperity, or other money-related teachings, money is a critical element in taking the gospel to the world, and I would urge you to consider your position on the issue.

Whatever choice you make, I suggest you move ahead with the utmost prayer, caution, and respect for the Word of God.

Principle #4:
You need to ask regularly

On their own, most people will not form a habit of giving to you. They will wait for you to ask. They will wait for a need to be shown. Left alone, they will respond only periodically or not at all.

I recently heard a minister say, "If God wants my ministry to prosper, He'll prosper it. If He wants it to fail, there's not much I can do about it."

Let's consider this approach for a moment.

If that applied to our health, we would never have to ask for medical treatment or advice. If it applied to our marriages, we would never have to work at that either.

I firmly believe that although God is sovereign and in control, when it comes to ministry, *there are things for us to do.* In the same way that there are techniques involved in building a house, driving a car, or

169

flying an airplane, there are techniques we need to know to properly present our ministries to the public, offering them an opportunity to stand with us in support.

The secret is to develop ways that do not interfere with the proper and ethical presentation of the gospel. The great balance is to give people the opportunity to give, and still be true to your mandate for ministry. The Bible teaches that God wants people to give. He also wants people to learn *how* to give—and how to encourage others to give. Fundraising, if it is anything, is systematic and periodic.

I don't believe you are justified in blaming God if your program doesn't stay on the air because of a lack of funds. If you choose not to ask people to support your work to further the gospel message, or ignore other important principles such as those presented throughout this book, that is your responsibility.

But on the other hand, if you abuse the principles of giving, or violate the trust your audience has in your ministry, your fate is equally sealed.

Some Questions and Answers

1) How big should a ministry be before it considers "fundraising"?

Every ministry and Christian organization should think about it. Even the smallest church in the most rural area can use the principles of giving to enhance its ministry and the work it is doing. We all have to pay our bills to keep the lights on, write salary checks, and stay in ministry.

I suggest you take the word *fundraising* out of your "scary" vocabulary and realize that it only means systematic, precise, and proven techniques for taking an offering. You properly prepare before you preach a sermon, the choir rehearses before they perform, and your organist practices before the service.

In the same way, you should properly prepare before you take an offering.

2) Don't you need large computers and printing presses before you can get into fundraising?

No. Start where you are, with the materials and equipment you have. It's amazing today what a simple personal computer can do.

3) Where can I get help in fundraising?

A number of organizations and firms make this their specialty. Even some colleges and universities have specialty departments or services that can provide fundraising advice for nominal fees. Once again, if you have an experienced producer or media consultant, they can guide you to a professional fundraiser. The best bet for your church or ministry is one of the numerous Christian fundraising organizations and companies across the country, since they are especially geared toward Christian television and radio ministries. The best list is the annual directory produced by National Religious Broadcasters, in Manassas, Virginia.

Avail yourself of information that will enable you to acquire the techniques of fundraising, even if it's from sources that aren't necessarily Christian in their orientation. You'll learn a number of skills that can readily adapt to your work.

But having said that, it's important to remember that a ministry fundraising effort is different from a secular effort. You should find a company that is sensitive to the gospel message, and understands the unique nature of this type of work. There are many Christian fundraising companies out there, and the best way to find them is to look at other ministries you respect and admire. Talk with other ministers or church leaders and ask their advice. They may recommend someone to you.

One last thing to consider in this area is "donor development." Some fundraisers attempt to squeeze every dollar out of your viewers all at once. In many cases, that specific fundraising project will yield a positive result, but you've probably exhausted your supporters for the future. A responsible fundraising expert understands how to develop your supporters and partners into becoming regular givers over the long haul. Most ministries would agree that a large number of people giving a small gift each month without fail is far better than a few giving large gifts on a very irregular basis. So look for someone who understands donor development and can implement a long-term plan for your financial growth.

4) How are fundraisers paid?

Most fundraisers are paid on a retainer basis. Usually they will want a contract for six months or a year. Be wary of those who ask for a percentage of the money they raise. This is not illegal, but many consider it unethical in the fundraising industry.

Believe in Your Ability to Raise Money

One of the essentials to successful fundraising is your belief in your ability to raise money. Of course God causes people ultimately to give, but you have to believe that your ministry is a worthy organization for people to give to.

From my observation, this belief arises from your commitment to the project you are doing, and your confidence in your own calling. Do you wholeheartedly believe in the ministry God has given you? (We're back to motivation and calling—see Chapter One). If so, this is a baby that you want to see grow and mature into adulthood. You'll want to give it the right nourishment and nurturing, and that takes an infusion of money.

If you don't fully believe in your project, it's difficult to muster your own belief that you personally can raise the millions of dollars that may be required to sustain the television ministry you desire.

Begin with your mission, your call, the projects that have arisen as a result of that call. Start there with your viewers. Show them why you care. Show them what compels you to action. Show them what you are doing.

Show, don't attempt to "snow" your partners, or eventually you'll get caught in drifts of your own creation.

I also urge you not to react to the abuses of others by deciding not to participate in fundraising. Many of my clients hesitate to ask for support on the air because of the terrible ways other pastors and evangelists have done it in the past (or are still doing it). There's no question that numerous people have given all of us a bad rap in this area, but I don't believe in *reacting;* I believe in *acting.* Just because others abuse their children, I still chose to have kids.

Let's take the high road here, and not deny our vision the finances it needs to survive because of the actions of others. Let's simply look for a better way.

What About Direct Mail?

In most cases, direct mail is the real workhorse of a fundraising campaign. The vast majority of television ministries use television as a vehicle for getting names of potential supporters, and then employ direct mail to actually raise the money.

That is certainly the case where ministries offer a *free gift* to the viewer. Other than getting the book, tape, or other gift into the audience's hands, the important thing here is to get the name and address. Then there can be follow-up through the mail and the viewer can be given the chance to become a regular ministry supporter or partner.

> **Important Note:** *Nearly every ministry audience has its own distinct personality. There are some ministries where offering a free gift always gets a great response. Other ministries get no response at all. Some always get responses using books, others with tapes, or other products. That's why it's so important to get in contact with a Christian professional who can evaluate your audience quickly—before you get into financial trouble.*

For instance, in my recent experience, when you offer a free gift, you'll probably get lots of calls and letters, but those people generally won't be very committed. They'll call for something free, but aren't very interested in really getting behind your ministry and supporting you financially.

Direct mail campaigns can be very obnoxious and you no doubt have seen many terrible examples. On the other hand, most churches and ministries use direct mail with great sensitivity and integrity. Either way, direct mail is still a standard technique for raising the necessary finances to keep a media ministry alive.

I do believe that even the smallest ministry can begin a productive direct mail outreach and probably should do so at the first opportunity. In fact, direct mail has been effectively employed numerous times to raise the initial funds necessary to begin a television outreach.

I would say a final word of caution in approaching ministry fundraising through television: *remember to use television as ministry, not just a way to market your ministry.*

Some ministries on the air today have forgotten their original roots in ministering to the needs of their audience, and are now using television primarily as a marketing tool for their ministries. As I said in an earlier chapter, in the best of all possible worlds we would never have to worry about financing our television programs and could concentrate solely on outreach. But since we obviously have to pay our bills, I advocate getting the best fundraising advice, and using it in a responsible manner with integrity, good judgment, and balance.

Chapter Eight

Radio

"You see, wire telegraph is a kind of a very, very long cat. You pull his tail in New York and his head is meowing in Los Angeles. Do you understand this? And radio operates exactly the same way: you send signals here, they receive them there. The only difference is that there is no cat."

Albert Einstein (1879 - 1955),
when asked to describe radio.

"My father hated radio and could not wait for television to be invented so he could hate that too."

Peter De Vries

Early in the 20th century, the famous radio preacher Dr. S. Parkes Cadman of Brooklyn, New York, addressed a great men's meeting in New Britain, Connecticut. The pastor, Theodore A. Greene, introduced the radio preacher with a sudden burst of oratory.

Dr. Greene told how he had been backstage at a large radio station and had seen all of the electrical equipment, the great batteries, generators, sparks flying, lights, and so forth. Increasing his remarks in tempo and volume, he suddenly cried:

"Think of the radio ministry of Dr. Cadman and his incredible ministry across the airwaves of the nation every Sunday afternoon, the millions who listen

spellbound! I introduce you to the king of the electrons, the ruler of the airways, in fact, the prince of the power of the air!"

I feel certain Dr. Greene had only been caught up in the sound of his own oratory in ascribing the title *"prince of the power of the air"* to this radio preacher—a title normally attributed to Satan—but the anecdote does serve to make a point: radio, for many years, had incredible power over the American mind and heart. And in many places around the world, including many places right here in the United States, it still does.

Since television came into widespread use, radio has been looked upon as something of a media stepchild. I don't believe that is an appropriate designation. Ministers have tended to shy away from radio, thinking it does not bring in the revenues of television, is not capable of maintaining a consistent high income, or that most people aren't listening. But the facts do not support these opinions.

- Americans do listen to radio—virtually every day. (Not as they did in "radio drama" days, to be sure, but they do listen.)
- Americans do support radio ministries, especially those that are on daily with a teaching message. Some of these ministries are actually among the most popular media programs today, and the personalities of radio are reemerging as some of the best-read authors of Christian books.

- The largest Christian association of broadcasters, the National Religious Broadcasters, was birthed out of radio, and today those involved in the radio industry represent its largest group of members.

I have rarely mentioned radio in previous chapters, but I could have easily included it in almost every chapter. Everything that has been said about finding a format, personnel, equipment, and so forth applies to radio as well as to television. Even fundraising techniques work as well on radio. If you are really interested in radio, I suggest you turn back through this book and insert the word "radio" just about every place you read "television."

I do want to make clear my opinion that the debate between television and radio is not an *either/or* situation. I don't think either one is *better or worse*. I happen to personally produce television programs because I especially enjoy the medium, and I am primarily a visual person.

But the fact is, television and radio are two equally important and valid tools with which to spread the gospel. Each has its own unique characteristics, and each should be examined in the light of those characteristics.

I am particularly frustrated at television ministers who simply strip the soundtrack from their television programs and use them on the radio. There's nothing *technically* wrong with that approach, except that it fails to recognize the peculiarity of radio, and therefore fails to exploit its strengths.

If you already have a television program and want to use your soundtrack on radio, perhaps you should certainly explore that possibility. That is definitely the least expensive and quickest way to cover both media with your message. But on the other hand, as you read this section of the book, keep in mind that radio has its own set of characteristics, and when you produce a program specifically for radio, your outreach can be so much more dynamic and fruitful.

Christian radio has the potential for being a great deal more than an edited section of last Sunday's sermon

How many times do you turn on the radio to hear, "Now let's join Pastor X in the service already in progress?" Radio has the potential for a great deal more creativity than that. Choose a format that works within your ministry in the same way you would choose a television format. Music? Preaching? Interviews? Variety? They all work on radio!

Diversity is the key to understanding the radio audience

In the last 20 years, radio has made many of the same changes as television, and there's at least as much diversity out there on the dial. In the past, you might have had a "pop" music station. Now you have *hard rock, light rock, heavy metal, oldies, easy listening, punk, adult rock, and on and on.*

Even the term *"contemporary Christian music"* has lost its meaning because of the many diverse styles now grouped within that category.

In radio, you'll want to "shop" for the right station even more carefully than for television

As of this writing, approximately 45 percent of the top 100 Christian stations in the nation are rated by an audience research company, and many stations have very well-researched profiles on their listeners. You'll want to shop for a station very carefully.

I think radio listeners tend to be more loyal to a particular station than television viewers. There's not nearly as much channel hopping to find a particular program of interest. Listeners tend to tune to a station and stay there. In reality, they may very well change stations, but they limit their options more than the typical cable-TV viewer. In other words, a radio listener is likely to have a few favorite radio stations, whereas a cable-TV viewer isn't loyal to a station, but is likely to choose a program in a particular time slot, no matter what station is airing it.

Radio is an especially effective way to reach young people

Many people think of young people as being glued to television sets. The greater likelihood is that they are plugged into radio receivers, especially during the teenage years. There are also some very exciting things being done right now to bring together Christian radio stations and Christian television programs to reach young people. In some cities, these media companies are joining together to produce MTV-style television programs and jointly simulcasting the soundtracks on the radio stations.

Radio is a project for which you may be able to raise funds through direct mail and through television

Rather than considering radio a *medium*, you may want to consider it a *project*. By that I mean a radio outreach is a wonderful project for getting support, especially when you lay out a very specific plan for reaching the lost. Here are just some of the factors that make radio a worthy project:

- Radio represents a project that reaches audiences not presently saturated with the gospel message—especially in developing nations.

- It is a good outreach to young people. For this reason, you'll need a good support base to catch that vision and pay the bills since those young people listening to the programs won't have the support dollars.

- It is a good outreach to the sick and shut ins. Many older folks still enjoy listening to the radio—especially those with poor vision.

- It is an excellent outreach for missions. Most of the world has radio and listens to radio regularly. Worldwide evangelism is especially possible through radio.

Like television, radio also can portray a project that has multiple facets for fundraising purposes

- Sponsorship for airtime for specific stations in different regions or nations.
- Sponsorship for the costs related to the production of the programs.
- Sponsorship for equipment (actual hardware and station necessities for missions projects) or specific projects.

Radio links well to print and direct mail aspects of a ministry.

As I mentioned earlier, a number of well-known and well-respected Christian authors today got their start (and remain today) as ardent radio personalities.

As one minister put it, "Radio is our audio track. Print and mail are our visual tracks. I suppose if you put them together, you might say we have an audio-visual ministry, and that's pretty close to a television ministry without the expense!"

For instance, it is easy to produce a bible study series on radio, and to have supplemental materials—study guides, books, and other literature—available through your direct mail outreach.

Radio has some distinct advantages over TV

- Radio programs are less expensive and faster to produce.
- Radio airtime is less expensive to buy.
- Radio lends itself to the creation of products that are actually a "recycling" of itself.

Stop and think about this for a moment. Audiocassettes of programs can be put together readily to make "teaching tape" sets, which is something that television is doing on a smaller scale. There are ministries that have had great success with videotape series. But audiotapes or CD sets are less expensive to record and produce, at least at the time of this writing. I do believe strongly in the future of videotape or DVD premiums; and as costs for videotapes and DVDs drop, and as more viewers purchase those players and become consumers, ministries will find an increased market for home video product.

- Radio doesn't care what you look like and that can have its advantages! Remember the old saying: "He has a face for radio."

Radio is actually a "hot" medium, as compared to television being a "cold" one. I realize these differences may be mostly semantic and academic, but the fact remains that,

Radio triggers the imagination

Radio can be used to make elephants fly! (At least in one's mind.) Thus, radio "involves" the listener in a way that television does not. Television is literal. What you see is what you get. Radio is limited only to the imagination.

Radio can be consumed more readily and in more places than television. On the beach, in your car, by a stream high in the mountains. In other words, you can take radio with you. Television is becoming increasingly portable, but it's still a few years behind the general use of the *boombox* or old *transistor radio*. And consider how many workplaces allow radios, but would never allow a television set.

Finally, as one last alternative, let's look at radio from another perspective.

Is there a way your present television programs might be slightly edited and used on radio to increase your audience, probably doubling that audience for much less than double the costs? In order to get the most out of the two media, is there a way your present television program might be adapted to radio format as an extension of your ministry?

Dream Interpretation!

Should you perhaps consider radio as an alternative medium for a particular aspect of your ministry—say your evangelistic outreach on television and your teaching outreach on radio?

The bottom line?

Don't miss radio. Its potential is vast. And there's lots of room for creativity and the ability to carve out your own market.

Chapter Nine

The Internet

"I am firmly of the opinion that the Macintosh is Catholic and that DOS is Protestant. Indeed, the Macintosh is counterreformist and has been influenced by the methodical path of the Jesuits. It is catechistic: the essence of revelation is dealt with via simple formulae and sumptuous icons. Everyone has a right to salvation. DOS is Protestant, or even Calvinistic. It allows free interpretation of scripture, demands difficult personal decisions, imposes a subtle hermeneutics upon the user, and takes for granted the idea that all can reach salvation."

Umberto Eco, Italian novelist.

"Internet is so big, so powerful and pointless that for some people it is a complete substitute for life."

Andrew Brown

The Internet is rapidly in the process of changing everything in Christian media. It has not developed as quickly as many had hoped, and we've already seen a record number of attempts to combine television with computers fall by the wayside. However, in most cases, that's because the number of consumers purchasing "broadband" connections has not grown as quickly as many would have liked.

"Broadband" simply means a "wider pipeline." In other words, a typical dial-up connection to the Internet limits the amount of data that

187

can flow through the phone line and into your computer. With new innovations like DSL, cable modems, satellite connections, and T-1 and higher lines, speeds are rapidly increasing, and it's becoming more and more common for people to view short films, commercials, and animation through their Internet connections.

In fact, as I write this draft of the manuscript, I'm on the road shooting a television project, and I'm sending versions back and forth to my office via wireless e-mail from my laptop computer. My wireless modem is a faster connection than the old dial-up I used to use in hotel rooms and airports across the country.

BMW Films (www.bmwfilms.com) was a real pioneer in creating short films for the Internet by taking advantage of these faster services. Created by the BMW automobile company, they hired big-time Hollywood directors to create dramatic short films—all designed around stories involving a BMW vehicle. Some were car chase stories, some were con artist tales, some were comedies, but all were very well-developed, photographed, and edited. The idea was a huge success. Literally millions of people have viewed the short films on the BMW website and the company had a fantastic marketing and advertising hit on their hands.

The point? People are finally coming around to watching TV programming on the Internet. Socially, we still have a way to go before the mass audience is ready to watch TV on their computers, but at least we're moving in that direction.

Home video companies like Blockbuster have already invested heavily into Internet distribution, and we're seeing signs of various companies developing technology that will allow us to download full-length movies into our computers. As a result, synergistic alliances with media companies, publishing firms, Internet distributors, and TV and movie studios are dramatically changing the face of the communications industry.

I use the BMW Films illustration to make an important point. Up to this point, most churches and ministries have used the Internet for publicity and advertising, directions to the church, announcements, or as a library to hold audio and video sermon clips from the pastor.

But this is just the tip of the iceberg.

If more churches and ministries could catch the vision of companies like BMW, and provide a wide selection and more creative array of options on the web, audiences would begin to respond more dramatically. Suppose you created a library of situations people face—depression, divorce, drug abuse, adultery, anger, financial problems, etc. When the viewer selects one of the categories, a short film appears that illustrates the problem, followed by a teaching lesson, and a follow-up study guide, book, or other resource. At that point, the web surfer could even interact with live web-based counselors. The options are virtually endless, and in each case, we'd be offering real answers to the real problems people face in life.

As of this writing, few people are willing to listen or view more than a few minutes of material from the web. Why? It's a cultural issue. There is far more to the media "environment" than most people realize. Where a person sits, what he or she is doing, or what the atmosphere is while enjoying media is a vital part of the experience. That's why people will watch movies in the living room on television, but aren't ready to view them on a computer or through a cell phone.

But know that the culture continues to move in that direction. In a world where you can watch TV on a cell phone, order plane tickets from your PDA, or buy a house on the Internet, anything is possible. As technology continues to change, we'll see new behaviors related to Internet viewing. As Christians, we need to stay abreast of these cultural changes in order to keep our message at the forefront of society and make it available to the widest possible audience.

As of this writing, one of the most significant cultural and technological changes we face is called "convergence." Convergence is the merging of various media technologies, and will eventually be the platform that completely changes the way we approach media and its impact on our lives.

Convergence - the next step in the digital age

Convergence. Everywhere we turn we hear about it—trade magazines, technical reports; there are even entire conferences dedicated to it. But what exactly does it mean, and how will it affect churches, ministries, and those of us in the Christian media world?

Simply put, "convergence" means looking at a single box. Today, information resources such as computers, and entertainment resources like television and radio have merged into a single unit. We can surf the web, do our computing, and watch the latest television program, all on the same piece of equipment.

In this context, the possibilities are nearly endless. A 1,000-channel universe? That's nothing in the world of convergence. For instance:

- The local video store will be a thing of the past—we can download any movie in existence as easy as downloading our e-mail.
- We can finally make television programs truly interactive.
- We can videoconference anywhere on the planet.
- We can add web hyperlinks into television programs to help people find out more information about any subject by accessing the web.
- We can find out immediate and accurate information about who's watching particular programs and why.
- Literally millions of music, movie, television program, website, and other entertainment choices will be at our fingertips.
- The list goes on and on…

Right now, numerous Hollywood studios, television networks, multimedia companies and others are working feverishly to make this concept of "convergence" happen. Other companies are trying to develop broadband video technology that will blend computers and television sets.

Each of these and a myriad of other companies are trying to do two things:

- Develop a creative entertainment format that people will want to view in the context of a computer environment.
- Develop the broadly accepted technology that will become the "VHS tape" if you will, of the industry. The company that develops the universally accepted technology that allows convergence to happen will reap billions financially.

But we keep coming back to the critical question, "What does this mean to Christians, and how can we be ready to use the new medium for presenting a message of hope to a world desperately in need?"

As a media producer and director, I'm not as concerned about the technology as I am with how we will use it. There are brilliant people that are working to create the technology. My interest is in how we as Christians will embrace the medium and use it to change the world. To accomplish that, I've created six "Keys" that we need to understand if we want to make an impact in the age of convergence. These are important principles that will help you create a more effective message within the context of this new medium, and help you cut through the clutter and advertising hype that surrounds the world of convergence.

Key #1 - For the secular audience, the media is today's pulpit

Growing up as a pastor's son in the South in the 1950s, I knew the moral climate of America was determined in the pulpit. But today, it's quite different. Today's moral climate is determined in TV studios, movie theaters and on the Internet. However, I find a remarkable number of pastors, evangelists, and church leaders are out of touch with today's culture. Don't believe me? Go on the web and use a search engine to find Christian youth sites. You won't believe the terrible websites you'll find. Some have excellent resources for young people, but their graphic presentation is so out-of-style, no young person would even consider looking at the site.

Producers often don't keep up with current programming and graphic styles, and I'm amazed at the number of Christian media professionals who never even watch television. If we're going to make an impact in this culture, we have to understand what makes it tick. Just as Paul in Acts 17 used his knowledge of Greek literature and culture to establish a "common ground" with the philosophers at Mars Hill, we need to understand the music, literature, films, and television that this culture creates. Otherwise, they will continue to believe that our message is irrelevant and unimportant. Remember, when it comes to the age of convergence, it's not worth doing if it's not done in a style and language this culture understands.

Key #2 - Make sure your financing is in place

Most Christian producers are plagued with a lack of funds for media production and equipment. Television, for instance, is probably the most expensive outreach your church or ministry will ever encounter, and poor decisions regarding financing can literally destroy an entire ministry organization. I always recommend that you have six months of funding in the bank before you ever began a new media outreach. On most basic cable systems today, there are a minimum of 70-plus channels, so it takes between six months and a year of broadcasting before your program begins to establish itself with your audience. In the world of convergence, the number of "channels" is potentially endless, and the competition is even greater. That means it could be months or years before you receive any significant prayer or financial support from your audience—they simply need time to find the program! Therefore, it's critical that you are able to fund your program at least during that first year, or your media ministry will never have the chance to make an impact.

Key #3 - Storytelling works—no matter what the medium

As far as I'm concerned, convergence isn't about equipment, it's about content. Of course we'll need the technology to bring these diverse media together, but it's the content that will decide its direction, impact, and legacy. That's why so many streaming media websites have failed—the technology was there, but they haven't figured out its most effective use.

As we enter the digital age of convergence, let's spend more time learning how to tell a story more effectively. It doesn't matter the program format—preaching, music, documentary, variety, drama, whatever. Every program is telling some type of story, and until that story is told most effectively, the audience is never going to be interested, and it's never going to translate to another medium.

There's no question that our storytelling abilities will be greatly challenged and expanded with the advent of convergence. The ability to move between the Internet and a television program, add a hyperlink to a movie, or integrate moving video into websites will allow us to tell our stories as never before. But don't allow links, transitions, and other gimmicks to distract us from the need to tell a story, and tell it effectively.

Essentially, it hasn't changed from the time Hebrew storytellers sat around campfires in the desert telling the stories that became the Old Testament.

The medium doesn't matter as much as the message.

In the coming age of convergence, let's make a new commitment to storytelling, and understand that unless we can tell a powerful and effective story, the delivery system won't matter.

Key #4 - Internet programming changes on a daily basis

The web is a fluid, changing environment—yet most Christian programming is predictable, and rarely changes. In Hollywood, millions of dollars are spent every year on "pilot" programs—many of which never see the light of day! The major studios and networks understand that audiences are always changing, so they aren't afraid to experiment and update programs and program ideas. But most Christian programs are doing the same thing they did 10-15 years ago, and most Christian websites rarely get updated. In the age of convergence, the most successful media ministries will be ministries who aren't afraid to change, update, and present a fresh, new approach to an ever-changing audience.

Key #5 - Don't let your vision stop at preaching

Preaching is a wonderful thing, and there will always be room in Christian media for good, solid preaching. But one of my greatest disappointments in Christian Internet sites is churches and ministries that just fill the site with video and audio clips of sermons. That's OK, but should only be the first step. We already know that Christian television has largely been a depository for videotaped sermons, but keep in mind our discussion that a church service doesn't necessarily make the best television program. Also, initial experience and research indicates that the Internet is largely used to "grab" different bits of information (or "factoids" as CNN calls them) from various sources.

Therefore, the audience isn't necessarily predisposed to sitting for 30-60 minutes to listen to a sermon—unless of course, its points are hyperlinked, there are visuals supporting the theme, and other ancillary graphics, destinations, and information, all linked to the sermon material.

Key #6 - Quality always transcends the medium

Many Christian churches and ministries don't understand the need to produce high quality media outreaches. But today's audiences are more technologically sophisticated than ever, and refuse to watch programs that aren't up to current standards of quality. Remember my earlier comment about most cable systems having at least 70 channels? And the unlimited channel universe is not far around the corner with the advent of convergence. In that environment, it's just too easy to change the channel or website if the picture, graphic style, or audio quality isn't satisfying.

Always remember—stewardship isn't necessarily saving money; it's using money more effectively. Sometimes that means spending more money to purchase a better product that will help you reach your goals sooner and more effectively.

Many churches and ministries purchase cheap equipment in order to save money—but soon discover they should have waited until they could afford better quality. Don't let your desire to get on radio, television or the Internet push you into getting low quality or inferior equipment. After all, you can't reach the lost if they won't watch long enough to hear your message.

Quality not only involves equipment, it involves people as well. Unqualified and unprofessional people never produce groundbreaking and effective work.

The issues of "convergence" can be both frightening and exhilarating at the same time. But if you will stay near the heart of God in your decision making, and seek the help and counsel of Godly men and women, as well as experienced media professionals, your chances of success will be greatly increased. God has given us the greatest message in the history of the world, and the baton has been handed to our generation—how committed are you to run the next leg of the race to win?

Chapter Ten

Conclusion

"From everyone who has been given much, much will be demanded; and from the one who has been entrusted with much, much more will be asked."

Luke 12:48

"God has not called us to be successful; He has called us to be faithful."

Jacques Maritain

Your effort to work through this book is an outstanding indicator of your desire not only to produce quality Christian television programs, but to do it right. Television production is not brain surgery. It's difficult, takes skill, and will demand your full attention, but the fact is, it can be done, and you can learn what it takes to do it well.

Being faithful to that calling and journey will be the key to learning what it takes to be triumphant. The more I learn in television and motion pictures, the more I realize there is much more to be learned.

But as you think about using television in your ministry, remember that what we might call *normal broadcast television programming* is only the tip of the media iceberg. In fact, many churches and ministries are involved extensively in television production and have never produced a program for actual broadcast.

Look at these other possibilities:

- ***Special Events***

A number of years ago a television ministry in Texas linked up via satellite with a large church in South Korea for a worldwide communion service.

In Africa, a few years later, using local television facilities, a feed was transmitted to Europe and linked instantly to the United States for joint broadcast of a worldwide crusade service.

In recent years, I've had the opportunity to be a part of major evangelistic crusades in Europe and the Caribbean where we transmitted via satellite those crusades each night to nearly a hundred separate countries. It was translated live into almost as many languages and featured music produced by each country's best Christian singers, singing in their own language. These programs weren't transmitted through local or national networks—they were directly transmitted to "downlink" sites in churches, auditoriums, movie theaters, and outdoor arenas.

The world can be reached and linked with television programs and video presentations just waiting to be created by you.

- ***Training, Motivational, & Archival Purposes***

You can use video as a training tool within your own church to improve your music programs, and worship services in the same way a football team watches game films to see what they can do better.

You can prepare videotapes for church visitors to provide an orientation, or guided tour of your church for newcomers, to present the full scope of your programs, and to provide training segments for various groups within your church body.

You can use it to promote a building campaign in small groups, house-to-house, or in services.

You can use it to enhance missionary fundraising drives. It's especially helpful when it can show a special report from the missionary's country. It sure beats the old well-worn slide show we all remember from our youth.

You may want to develop a videotape library within your church featuring many of the fine Christian movies, teaching materials, and children's videos on the market.

You can use it to train choirs or performance groups.

You can use it to document important events in the life of your church or ministry for historical and archival reasons.

You can use it as an outreach to shut-ins and the sick.

You can use it in your educational programs, Sunday school, and Bible studies. It's an excellent means for a pastor to visit all of the "cell groups" in his church during any given week or month.

One church client of mine sends about 100 videotapes to missionaries each month around the globe.

There are thousands of ideas waiting to be turned into reality. And virtually any and all of them can be done successfully.

Where do I go from here?

In each section of this book, I have tried to direct you to the types of people who can help you prepare for your future television ministry. Looking to other, more experienced ministries for advice, professional media consultants, local businessmen who have dealt with buying TV time, local production companies who know Christian freelancers in your area, and even Christian colleges and universities with film and television departments can provide the high-quality sources of information that you need.

Involvement in the National Religious Broadcasters is perhaps the most effective way to get your television ministry off the ground. Through their monthly magazine NRB, annual national conventions, an directory of members and services, and many other resources, the National Religious Broadcasters is an outstanding source for media consultants, program producers, advertising agencies, consulting firms, direct mail firms, and others.

Keep in mind, some Christian producers, organizations, and firms are not members of the NRB and will not be listed there. But there is no question that the NRB is certainly the most effective and comprehensive place to start.

And remember my earlier advice: get professional counsel from people who have been there. Whether legal, fundraising, or production, every single step of the way. This advice alone will make a major difference in your success.

Phil Cooke

Appendix

A Reading List for Further Study

I'm saddened at how little Christian TV stations, churches, and ministries involved in television, know about the history and techniques of television and motion pictures. You can't believe how often producers or directors will call me with some new method they think they've just invented and I pull a book from my library and show them that someone was already doing it back in 1955.

It's no different than a concert pianist not knowing anything about Bach or Beethoven, or a great pastor not knowing about men like Augustine, Luther, Wesley, Finney, Moody, or others.

At my workshops and seminars around the world I'm constantly quoting famous producers and directors, or telling historic incidents from the early days of secular or Christian television. I strongly believe that *until we know where we've come from, we'll never know where we are, and we certainly won't know where we're going.*

Learn more, not only about the history of television and motion pictures, but how the media has impacted our culture as well. It will open your mind to a world of new ideas and possibilities.

Research is another area that we don't explore nearly enough. The secular networks and Madison Avenue spend hundreds of millions of dollars a year on research to find out who their audience is and how to more effectively reach them. We need to understand that good research doesn't hinder creativity or anointing; it simply gives us the tools we need to learn how to focus that creativity and anointing where it will do the most good.

I will divide this appendix into reference materials that will help you in the actual day-to-day production of the television programs. Then I will give you an additional reference section that will help you expand your knowledge of the media and how it is shaping the world we live in.

Many of these books have been classics for years and are updated on a regular basis. When you contact your local bookstore (or the bookstores I suggest later), be sure and ask for the latest version. Also, because of the nature of trade publications and industry books, some will be out of print, and of course more are being written. Use this chapter as a guide, but always be looking for new resources and material. If you do find some are out of print, I recommend you investigate out-of-print book search sites on the Internet.

I do not necessarily agree with everything in these books, but I do believe they are some of the most informative on the market today.

The Basic List

This is a basic reading list that I hand out at my media conferences. I think for an overall understanding of media and its influence on our society, this is a great place to start. It also covers books that will help you become a leader in your media ministry.

Carnegie, Dale - *How to Win Friends & Influence People*—Pocket Books

Maxwell, John - *Developing The Leader Within You*—Thomas Nelson

Maxwell, John - *The 17 Essential Qualities Of A Team Player Becoming The Kind Of Person Every Team Wants*—Thomas Nelson

Maxwell, John - *Becoming A Person Of Influence*—Thomas Nelson

Downs, Tim. *Finding Common Ground How to communicate with those outside the Christian community...While we still can*—Moody Press

Van Oech, Roger - *A Kick in the Seat of the Pants*—Perennial Library

Ford, Leighton. *The Power of Story: Rediscovering the Oldest, Most Natural Way to Reach People for Christ* - NavPress

Hahn, Todd and David Verhaagen. *Reckless Hope: Understanding and Reaching Baby Busters*—Baker Books

Johnston, Robert K. *Reel Spirituality: Theology and Film in Dialogue*—Baker Books

Romanowski, William D. *Pop Culture Wars: Religion & the Role of Entertainment in American Life*—InterVarsity Press

Roof, Wade Clark. *A Generation of Seekers: The Spiritual Journeys of the Baby Boom Generation*—HarperCollins Publishers

Smith, J. Walker and Ann Clurman. *Rocking the Ages: The Yankelovich Report on Generational Marketing*—HarperCollins Publishers, Inc.

Stone, Bryan P. *Faith and Film: Theological Themes at the Cinema*—Chalice Press

Webster, Douglas D. *Selling Jesus: What's Wrong with Marketing the Church*—InterVarsity Press

Television Program Production

One of the oldest and most complete library style collections of books I have seen is from Hastings House Publishers in New York. I suggest you send for a catalogue under the title *"Communication Arts Books"*. Some of the titles are as follows:

The Technique of Television Production, by Gerald Millerson

The Technique of the Television Cameraman, by Peter Jones

The Technique of Television Announcing, by Bruce Lewis

The Technique of the Sound Studio, by Alec Nesbitt

The Technique of Lighting for Television and Motion Pictures, by Gerald Millerson

The Technique of Film and Television Make-up, by Vincent J.R. Kehoe

Other Practical Television References:

Television Production Handbook, by Herbert Zettl—Wadsworth Publishing Company

The Television Program, It's Direction And Production, by Edward Stasheff and Rudy Bretz—Hill and Wang

A Sense of Direction - by William Ball—Drama Book Publishers

Directing Your Directing Career by K. Callan—Sweden Press

Tinker in Television, by Grant Tinker & Bud Rukeyser—Simon & Schuster

Television and Radio, by Giraud Chester, Garnet R. Garrison, Edgar E. Willis—Appleton-Century-Crofts, Meredith Corp.

Stage Scenery, by A.S. Gillette—Harper and Row

Producing and Directing for Television, by C. Adams—Holt

Getting Your Message Out; How To Get, Use, And Survive Radio And Television Airtime, by Michael M. Klepper—Prentice Hall, Inc.

The Craft of Interviewing, by John Brady—Writer's Digest Books

Videotape Recording: Theory and Practice, by J.F. Robinson—Hastings House

This Business of Music, Sidney Shemel and M. William Krasilovsky—Billboard Books

Television, Michael Winship—Random House

Off-Hollywood - The Making and Marketing of Independent Films, by David Rosen—Grove Weidenfeld.

The Movie Business Book, edited by Jason E. Squire—Simon & Schuster.

Writing for Television

Story - by Robert McKee—Harper Collins

The Writer's Resource Guide, edited by William Brohaugh—Writer's Digest Books

Writing Television and Radio Programs, by F.F. Willis—Holt, Rinehart and Winston

Video Scriptwriting, by Barry Hampe—Plume Books

The Writer and The Screen, by Rolf Rilla—William Morrow & Company

An American Rhetoric, by W.W. Watt—Holt, Rinehart and Winston

The Art of Fiction; Notes on Craft For Young Writers, by John Gardner—Knoft

The Complete Guide to Standard Script Formats, by Judith Haag and Hillis Cole Jr.—CMC Publishing

Advertising and Promotion

Contemporary Advertising, by Courtland L. Bovee and William F. Arens—Irwin

Response Television, by John Witek—Crain Books

Marketing Channels, by Craig R. Evans—Prentice Hall

Inventing Desire, by Karen Stabiner—Simon & Schuster

Motivation in Advertising, by Pierre Martineau—McGraw-Hill

How To Produce an Effective TV Commercial, by Hooper White—Crain Books

Positioning: The Battle for Your Mind, by Al Ries and Jack Trout—McGraw-Hill Books

Subliminal Seduction, by Wilson Bryan Key—Signet Books, New American Library

Corporate Advertising, by Thomas Garbett—McGraw-Hill

Advertising Copywriting, by Philip Ward Burton—Grid Publishing, Inc.

Direct Response Broadcast and New Electronic Media, edited by Karen Burns—Direct Mail Marketing Association

Successful Direct Marketing Methods, by Robert Stone—Crain Books

The following references will be an invaluable source of information:

Hollywood Reporter Blue-Book Directory,
www.hollywoodreporter.com

Although it features companies based in Los Angeles, this will list everything from studios, make-up artists, post-production facilities, and stock footage houses. Even if you are in another part of the country, this is still an important reference for stock footage, post-production, special graphics and effects, and other aspects of production. This is a must-have book for any serious production office.

The Business of Television
Howard J. Blumenthal and Oliver R. Goodenough
(Billboard Books, NY)
This is one of the most comprehensive books I have seen on the business aspect of television. It has a terrific reference section including model contracts, memos, and other standard forms.

Advertising Agency Information via the Internet:

www.adweek.com
www.crain.com
www.adage.com
www.adcritic.com

Directory of Religious Broadcasting

The National Religious Broadcasters is a national organization that represents the interests of the religious broadcasters in America. It publishes a regular magazine called: "NRB," and is the national voice for many issues relating to Christian radio, television, and other media.

This reference lists Christian television and radio program producers, advertising agencies, direct mail consultants, television and radio stations, and many other important areas within Christian television. Along with the Studio Blue-Book, this is a must-have reference for a serious Christian program producer.

www.nrb.org.

The Producer's Masterguide

www.producers.masterguide.com

A similar directory to the Hollywood Reporter Blue-Book.

Professional and Governmental Organizations:

American Society of Composers, Authors & Publishers

One Lincoln Plaza

New York, NY 10023

212-621-6000

www.ascap.com

also:

ASCAP—LA

7920 W. Sunset Blvd. Third Floor

Los Angeles, CA 90046

323-883-1000

Broadcast Music, Inc.

320 W. 57th St.

New York, NY 10019

212-586-2000

www.bmi.com

American Association of Advertising Agencies

405 Lexington Avenue, 18th Floor

New York, NY 10174

212-682-2500

www.aaaa.org

Federal Communications Commission

Consumer Assistance and Small Business Offices

Federal Communications Commission

445 12th Street SW

Washington, DC 20554

1-888-CALL-FCC (1-888-225-5322)

www.fcc.gov

Television and Culture

The following list is by no means exhaustive, but it will help you begin to expand your knowledge on culture, the media, and their implications for our lives today. As you explore these books, continue to be on the lookout for other similar and insightful books.

What Americans Believe—by George Barna. George Barna has done some outstanding research into giving us a clearer picture of America, and especially market profiles of the Christian community. His company, the Barna Research Group in Glendale, California has conducted extensive research for both secular and Christian organizations. This is another must for a Christian television producer.

George Barna has done other books such as *Virtual America*, and his *Barna Reports* series. They are all excellent resources, and I would suggest you ask for his latest books

Culture Wars: The Struggle to Define America—by Ken Myers - A book that deals with these issues on an up-to-the-minute basis. Most interesting because of its unique approach to certain cultural issues.

Air of Salvation - The Story of Christian Broadcasting, by Mark Ward Sr. An excellent perspective on the history of Christian broadcasting in America.

A Generation of Seekers, by Wade Clark Roof. An excellent reference work on the spiritual journeys of the baby boom generation.

Children at Risk - Dr. James Dobson and Gary Bauer - Long a traditional marriage and family icon, Dr. Dobson explores the dangers of growing up in today's society. Although especially written for parents, its informative chapters on art, entertainment options, and the media will help in your decision-making about what is best for your children.

Christ and the Media - Malcolm Muggeridge - This is a wonderful little book for everyone who has even the slightest interest in the world of television. Based on a series of lectures, it raises intriguing questions about how we express our faith through the media, and whether or not the price may be too high.

Every producer of Christian programs in America should have a well worn copy of this book on his or her nightstand.

Hollywood Priest - Ellwood Kieser - The first-hand account of Father Ellwood Kieser's founding of Paulist Productions, creators of the network series *Insight*, and his more recent foray into producing major motion pictures. A fascinating story of a Catholic Priest's struggle to shape the values of America through quality television and motion pictures.

Modern Art & the Death of a Culture - H.R. Rookmaaker - This is not light reading. It's an insightful and in-depth look at the history of art and its culmination in the modern art movement of today. The ramifications of that movement are then refracted through the lens of Christian perspective and the author achieves some insightful conclusions.

The Plug-In Drug - Marie Winn - This is the result (now revised) of a groundbreaking study of television, children, and the family. Unlike many researchers who concentrate on the programming aspect of television watching (what types of programs they view), Winn explores the impact of just the passive act of watching television for hours on end. It will definitely make you re-examine your attitudes on how much television your children watch.

Amusing Ourselves to Death - Neil Postman - This is one of my current favorites, although Postman is certainly not writing from a Christian perspective. This is an excellent examination of communication in the age of show business. Although we disagree on certain points, I believe his direction is to be applauded. Similar to Winn, he doesn't worry so much about the content of programs, but the actual act of watching. In fact, he isn't so much concerned about the idiotic programs *(Jerry Springer, Survivor, Who Wants to Marry My Dad)* which we readily acknowledge to be garbage, but shows like *60 Minutes, Dateline, and Eye-witness News*, where people actually believe what they are seeing.

One Nation Under Television, The Rise & Decline of Network TV - J. Fred Macdonald - This is an excellent book. I almost read it in one sitting. For a historical perspective on network television, and valuable insight into the process, it's hard to beat.

Remote Control - Frank Mankiewicz - This was published in the late seventies, but has some interesting information and research on topics like TV violence, family viewing, news, and racial issues on television.

Inside Prime Time - Todd Gitlin - For those who don't understand much about the behind-the-scenes world of network television, this is an excellent background text. More up-to-date than most, it's a good book for trying to understand how prime time evening slots are programmed.

Four Arguments for the Elimination of Television - Jerry Mander - A classic work that came out of the 1970s, this raises some good arguments, although his basic premise of eliminating television is unrealistic. I love reading it. It makes a lot of sense, and will really make you think.

Walking on Water: Reflections on Faith and Art - Madeleine L'Engle - This is one of those books that I mark in over and over again. A great source of encouragement to the Christian artist, and an even better source of information for others on how a Christian artist functions, and receives his or her inspiration. I also recommend reading Madeleine L'Engle's novels including *A Wrinkle in Time, A Swiftly Tilting Planet,* and *A Wind in the Door.*

There are many other books available about producing and broadcasting television programs, and it would be impossible to list them all here. I would recommend you contact your local bookstore, or call an industry bookstore like the *Samuel French Bookshops* in Los Angeles. Samuel French has a very large collection of practical, how-to books related to television, home video, and motion pictures. They publish a frequent catalog, so call them and get on their mailing list.

Samuel French Bookshops
www.samuelfrench.com
818-762-0535 - Studio City, CA
323-876-0570 - Hollywood, CA

Industry Magazines and Journals

As a Christian producer, you don't have to bury yourself in trade journals and industry publications, but it's at least important to scan through to see what equipment, production techniques, and styles are current. Many of these magazines are free to professional producers, so drop them a line and at least get on their mailing list. You'll find they are a great source for stock footage, film commissions, tips, equipment reviews, and other information.

General Production:

Film & Video Magazine
www.filmandvideomagazine.com

Millimeter Magazine
www.millimeter.com

Backstage (For actors)
www.backstage.com

Update Magazine (Filming locations)
www.updatemag.tv

Videography
www.videography.com

Post Magazine
www.postmagazine.com

Television Week
www.crain.com

Media Week Magazine

www.mediaweek.com

New Media Magazine

www.newmedia.com

Broadcasting & Cable

www.broadcastingandcable.com

The Hollywood Reporter

www.hollywoodreporter.com

Billboard Magazine

www.billboard.com

Daily Variety

www.variety.com

Creativity Magazine

www.adcritic.com

Advertising Age

www.adage.com

Emmy Magazine

(The Academy of Television Arts & Sciences)

www.emmys.org

Professional and Media Related Religious Publications:

NRB Magazine

(National Religious Broadcasters)

www.nrb.org

Technologies for
Worship Magazine

www.tfwm.com

Church Production Magazine

www.churchproduction.com

Ministries Today Magazine

www.ministriestoday.com

Infomercial Production:

Response TV

www.responsemag.com

Home Video:

Video Business Online

www.videobusiness.com

Music Libraries

These music libraries are "buy-out" libraries which means you pay for the music once, and never again. I think it's the best way to begin to build a music collection for your programs and the price is definitely right. There are many other good libraries, so I recommend you search them out and ask for a demo tape and catalog.

Creative Support Services
www.cssmusic.com

Fresh Music
www.freshmusic.com

The Music Bakery
www.musicbakery.com

State Television and Film Commissions

A very valuable resource that not many Christian broadcasters use is their own state film commissions. A number of years ago, when states started to realize the positive economic impact of having a motion picture or television program produced locally, they began to establish offices to help lure more television and film production into the state.

Today, these offices are very sophisticated and can help you find equipment companies, freelance crew members, shooting locations, studios, and many other items.

Their services are free to the producer, and they are more than happy to help. Their goal is to encourage more production in your state, so my advice is to talk with their office as soon as possible.

Chances are, they won't be particularly sensitive to what you as a Christian ministry are trying to do, but for the practical aspects of television production, they can be a great help. A list of state and global film commissions can be found by subscribing or contacting *Location Update Magazine*—www.updatemag.tv.

Author's Note: The publications, references, and other services listed in this book are provided as a resource only. The writer and publisher are not responsible for any service or information listed, or connected in any way with these companies. Please use normal caution in dealing with anyone in respect to your television ministry, and use professional advice and counsel at all times.

Glossary

This glossary is not meant to be an exhaustive list of television words and phrases, but it hopefully will make you a little more familiar with some of the most often used television terms. Many of the reference books on television and the media listed in the last chapter will have much more complete glossaries and should be consulted.

Above-the-line costs: Production costs within a budget related to story, script, producer, director, and performers. The program's other costs are designated as "below the line."

AD: Assistant Director

Ad-Hoc Networks: A temporary grouping of stations created to carry a specific program.

Ad-lib: Unrehearsed dialog or action.

ADI: Area of Dominant Influence. The ratings services' term for the region in which local stations signals are dominant (corresponds to DMA).

Affiliate: A broadcast station not owned by a network, but airing its programs and commercials.

Phil Cooke

Ancillary markets: Secondary sales targets for a program that has completed its first run(s) on its initial delivery medium. For instance, after a network program airs, it will go to its ancillary markets, such as cable, home video, overseas, etc.

Aspect ratio: Proportional dimensions of the TV screen. Measures 3 units by 4 units (designated 3:4) by current standards, although the high definition standards will dramatically change everything.

Audio: The sound portion of the TV program.

Audio level: The strength of the audio signal.

Backlight: Direct illumination from behind the subject. This helps to define the subject and distinguish it from the background.

Back time: Figuring the amount of time left in a show or segment by subtracting the present time from the program end time.

Barn doors: Metal doors or flaps attached to the lights to help define and block the light.

Bars: Standard color test signal recorded at the beginning of a videotape in order to properly adjust playback machines.

Barter syndication: A program distribution method in which the syndicator retains and sells a portion of the show's advertising time. In *cash plus barter*, the syndicator also receives some money from the station on which the programs air.

Basic cable: Channels received by cable subscribers at no extra charge, usually supported by advertising and small per-subscriber fees paid by cable operators. At this time, religious networks are a part of basic cable coverage.

BetaSP: A professional broadcast format very commonly used. As of this writing, most remote location work is produced on BetaSP, but is rapidly moving toward the digital "DV" formats.

Blocking: Working out talent and camera positions for a production. Usually done by the director.

Board: The name for the sound console or sound mixer.

Break-up value: Or private market value, the estimated worth of a company when the assets are sold. Often, stations are sold off when a major group owner liquidates or sells.

Bumper: Graphic or visual used in the beginning or end of program segments to separate sections of the program.

0

C-band: The range of frequencies from four to six gigahertz (billion cycles per second) used by most communications satellites.

Camera Unit: The entire piece of video machinery used by the camera operator—the camera head, mount, tripod or pedestal, and the base.

Character generator: A computer that produces graphics for television programs, such as names, scripture references, etc. Today's character generators are very sophisticated and are often components of larger 3-D graphics and animation systems.

Churn: A cable industry rate based on a formula that takes into account the number of subscriber connects, disconnects, upgrades, and downgrades.

Clip: A short piece of videotape used in a program.

Closed captions: A form of teletext for hearing-impaired viewers that superimposes subtitles on programs and requires special decoders for reception.

Common carrier: The FCC's class of transmission systems, such as telephone, telegraph, and certain satellites, open to public use at uniform fees and generally not permitted to control content.

Contrast ratio: The difference between the darkest and brightest areas on the set or picture.

Control room: Where the director and production personnel control the audio and video for a program.

CPM: Advertiser's cost per thousand viewers exposed to a commercial.

Crossfade: Simultaneously fading one sound or picture in and another sound or picture out.

DAT: Digital Audio Tape, an audiocassette format available with very high quality recording capabilities.

DBS: Direct Broadcast Satellite.

DMA: Designated Market Area, a viewing region defined by Nielsen Media Research (corresponds to ADI which was used by Arbitron).

Downlink: To receive from a satellite, also the term for the dish actually used for the reception.

Dubbing: Transferring sound or video (or both) from one tape to another. Making a copy.

Fill light: Diffused light that is used to lessen shadows and harsh lines.

Frequency response: The range of frequencies that a piece of equipment is sensitive to and capable of accepting or reproducing.

Freeze-frame: To stop action on a videotape as in a still photograph.

Graphics: Visuals (usually words on the screen) prepared for a production.

Grazing: The act of constantly flipping through TV channels, watching several shows at once, brought on by the ease of remote-control units and the wider viewing selection that cable-TV offers. *Zapping* is a similar action used to skip over the commercials during a program.

HDTV: High-definition TV, various technical systems providing a finer and wider TV picture, usually with twice as many scanning lines as the standard TV which gives far greater picture resolution.

HUT: Homes Using Television, the percentage of TV homes with one or more sets in use at a given time.

In the can: A finished production—produced, edited, and ready to broadcast.

Jump cut: A jarring or unnatural transition between two shots. Usually because the shots are too similar.

Key light: The primary source of direct light on a subject. Often positioned at about a 45-degree angle from the subject.

Location: A production site or location outside a television studio.

Low-power TV: TV stations licensed by the FCC to use low transmitter power, usually in areas not locally served by full-power stations.

Major market: One of the 50 largest metro areas in numbers of TV households.

Master: The original tape. Similar terms: *Camera Master* - The camera originals. *Edited Master* - The edited master tape. *Dupe Master* - The master tape used to duplicate the program. (This is never the edited master in case it is damaged during duplication.)

MSO: Multiple System Operator, a company that operates more than one cable TV system.

Network: A program distributor interconnected with stations under different ownership for simultaneous broadcast. A narrower FCC definition says a network distributes at least 15 hours of programming a week to at least 25 affiliates in at least 10 states.

Pan: Movement of the camera in a left or right direction.

Pay cable: A program service supported by optional extra subscriber fees.

Pay-per-view: Programs purchased by subscribers on a per-program basis.

Penetration: In a given population, the percentage of households using a product or receiving a service.

Pre-production: The stage of production where a program is planned and prepared.

Prime-time: In practice, the three evening hours (four on Sunday) programmed by the broadcast networks, 8 to 11 PM Eastern and Pacific time, and 7 to 10 PM Central and Mountain time, Monday through Saturday, starting an hour earlier on Sunday.

Rating: Estimated percentage of the universe of TV households tuned to a program at once.

Reach: Percentage of audience exposed to an ad or program in a given period.

Rep firm: A company that sells time on local stations ("spot time") to national advertisers.

Resolution: Measure of a picture's detail. Horizontal lines of resolution in TV are counted across the screen.

RF microphone: A wireless microphone. Refers to *radio frequency*.

Rundown: A brief outline of the program for reference, in contrast to a complete script. A rundown lists segment order and times for each segment, but not actual dialogue.

Share: Estimated percentage of "HUT" watching a program.

Spot time: Commercial advertising time on a local station purchased from the station or rep firm.

State-of-the-art: The most current equipment and techniques available at that moment. Usually describes the latest technology on the market. A term often used flippantly and inaccurately as a way to impress the uninitiated.

Superstation: A local TV station whose signal is satellite delivered to cable systems across the country.

Take: The individual shots, scenes, or segments recorded on the videotape.

Tally light: A small red light on the camera that, when lit, tells the operator or talent that his camera is on the air.

Tilt: Camera movement that is up or down.

Transponder: A satellite component that receives and re-transmits a TV signal or perhaps many narrower-band data channels.

Truck: Movement of the entire camera unit either left, right, backward or forward.

TVRO: Television Receive Only - a satellite dish that can only receive signals, like the one in a backyard.

VHS: Video Home System - the leading consumer videocassette format. VHS uses half-inch videotape.

Voice-over: The off-camera announcer's voice.

Wacky-cam: A shooting style typified by floating or jerky camera movements. Most often used in music videos, or contemporary commercials. Designed to portray a free-floating, off the cuff, gritty feeling for the viewer. **NOTE:** There is a definite technique to this directing style. It's not just random jerking of the camera around, and you can tell when it really works.

Window: The period a network, station, or other distributor has the rights to show a program.

Zapping: Changing the channel by remote-control to avoid commercials.

Zipping: Fast-forwarding through commercials when playing back a program on your VCR.

Phil Cooke

Getting Help

Phil Cooke, President and CEO of Phil Cooke Pictures is one of the most successful and respected media consultants in Christian media today. He is also an award-winning commercial, music video, television and film producer and director, whose work has been profiled in the *Wall Street Journal*, *The New York Times*, and *The Los Angeles Times*. Selected projects have been placed in the permanent archive on the History of Broadcasting at the Newhouse School of Communication at Syracuse University representing landmark work in religious and inspirational broadcasting. He also lectures at numerous media conferences, universities and workshops, and has recently taught directing techniques as far away as Russia and Central America.

Dr. Cooke also has a Ph.D. in Theology, writing a doctoral dissertation titled, *Through a Glass Darkly: Revelation as a New Paradigm for Understanding Modern Cinema*.

Whether you are just beginning a new outreach or have been producing programs for years, Phil Cooke Pictures can help you isolate your trouble spots, polish your existing program, or create a new one altogether, and get you moving back on the road to success.

Working with an outside producer or media consultant can sometimes be an expensive process, but moving ahead with wrong or inadequate advice can be far more expensive and damaging. Through a network of experienced Christian producers, directors, and crew members across the country, Phil Cooke Pictures can help you get back on track and discover your potential in television.

Write, call, or e-mail Phil Cooke Pictures and let us know your situation. It will be helpful if you outline your situation on paper beforehand and, if possible, send a VHS cassette of your current program for reference.

The problem may be solved through a conference, a closer look at your facility, or contact with a producer or advisor who can take an active role in helping reshape your program.

Either way, Phil Cooke Pictures would like to be of service.

**PHIL
COOKE
pictures
INCORPORATED**

P.O. Box 1515
Burbank, CA 91507
Phone: (818) 563-2125
Fax: (818) 563-3662

The Phil Cooke Pictures World Wide Web site is:

www.cookefilm.com

It is designed to be a valuable resource for Christian media producers, featuring articles on television subjects, production tools, and helpful links to the best and most informative Internet sites for producers.

About the Author

Phil Cooke is an internationally known media consultant and award winning television writer and director, who's work has been profiled in the Wall Street Journal, The New York Times, and The Los Angeles Times. He is a respected media and production consultant for networks, studios, and major religious organizations. Projects written and directed by Phil Cooke have been placed in the permanent archive on the history of broadcasting at the Newhouse School of Communication at Syracuse University representing landmark work in inspirational and religious programming. A rare combination of entertainment professional and Ph.D., he also lectures at media conferences, and teaches writing and directing techniques in the United States, Europe, and Central and South America.